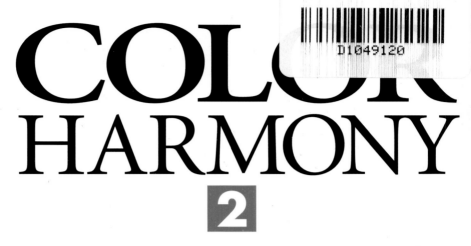

COLOR HARMONY 2

A GUIDE TO CREATIVE COLOR COMBINATIONS

Bride M. Whelan

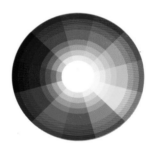

First printing, 1997

First published in the United States of America
in 1994 by:
Rockport Publishers, Inc.
146 Granite Street
Rockport, Massachusetts 01966
Telephone: (508) 546-9590
Fax: (508) 546-7141

Distributed to the book trade and art trade
in the U.S. by:
North Light, an imprint of
F & W Publications
1507 Dana Avenue
Cincinnati, Ohio 45207
Telephone: (513) 531-2222

First published in Germany, Austria,
Switzerland, and Scandinavia in 1994 by
Rockport Publishers for:
Gingko Press GmbH
Hamburgerstrasse 180
2000 Hamburg 76 Germany
Telephone: (40) 291 425
Fax: (40) 291 055

First published in India in 1994 by
Rockport Publishers for:
India Book Distributors
107/108, Arcadia, 195
Nariman Point
Bombay, 400 021 India

First published in Thailand in 1994 by
Rockport Publishers for:
Asia Books Co., Ltd.
5 Sukhumvit Soi 61
Sukhumvit Road
P.O. Box 40
Bangkok 10110 Thailand
Telephone: (662) 391-0590, 391-2680
Fax: (662) 391 2277, 381-1621

First published in Indonesia in 1994
by Rockport Publishers for:
Toko Buku Harapan
Komplex Loka Indah D-72
J1 Mangga Besar Ix
Jakarta 11170 Indonesia

First published in Korea in 1994
by Rockport Publishers for:
Dongnam Books Trading Company
Dongnam Building
#25-9, 1-ga, Choongmu-ro
Jung-gu
CPO Box 1275
Seoul Korea
Telephone: (02) 755 8303 - 5
Fax: (02) 755 5686

First published in the Philippines in 1994
by Rockport Publishers for:
National Bookstore
701 Rizal Avenue
Manila, Philippines

First published in Singapore in 1994
by Rockport Publishers for:
Page One—The Bookshop Pte Ltd
Blk 4, Pasir Panjang Road
#08-33 Alexandra Distripark
Singapore 0511
Telephone: (65) 273 0128
Fax: (65) 273 0042

First published in the U.K. and Australia in 1994
by Rockport Publishers for:
Thames and Hudson
30 Bloomsbury Street
London England WC1B 3QB

Other Distribution by:
Rockport Publishers, Inc.
Rockport, Massachusetts 01966

1-56496-401-9

Color Harmony 2 was imaged at FinalCopy,
Newburyport, Massachusetts, with 175-line
screens at 3386dpi on Anitec HNF film. Screen
tolerances were maintained at ± 1% as measured
with an X-Rite 341 transmission densitometer
and an X-Rite 418 color reflection densitometer.
Color proofs from the film positive process color
separations were made with Hoechst Pressmatch
Dry proofing material.

Printed in Hong Kong.

10 9 8 7 6 5 4 3 2 1

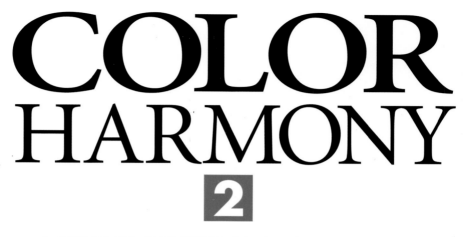

COLOR HARMONY 2

A GUIDE TO CREATIVE COLOR COMBINATIONS

Bride M. Whelan

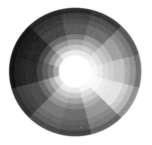

Rockport Publishers, Inc. Rockport, Massachusetts
Distributed by North Light Books,
Cincinnati, Ohio

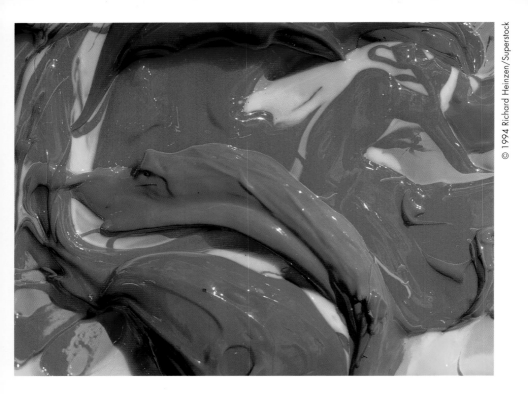

ACKNOWLEDGMENTS

Rockport Publishers would like to express their appreciation to Kristopher Hill and the staff at FinalCopy of Newburyport, Massachusetts, for their technical expertise, patience, and hard work in making this color book a reality, and also to Margaux King for her diligent photo research.

ABOUT THE AUTHOR

Bride M. Whelan, an instructor at Parsons School of Design, New York City, teaches basic and advanced courses in color theory. For many years she taught graphic design at Paier College of Art, New Haven, Connecticut, and lectures extensively on a variety of design-related topics.

Table of Contents

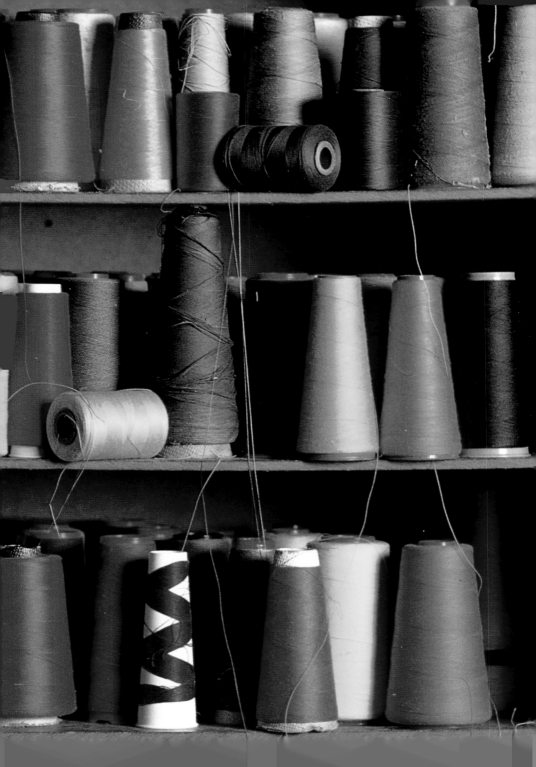

Introduction

Color affects our life.
Color is physical . . . we see it.
Color communicates . . . we receive
   information from the language of color.
Color is emotional . . . it evokes our feelings.

Ideas can be communicated through color without the use of either written or verbal language, and emotional response to individual colors alone or in combination is often predictable. For instance, a prestigious law firm sends a message of confidence to potential clients by using rich, deep colors in its office and on its letterhead. Conversely, a dentist's waiting area in bright red or orange sends a stressful message to patients, rather than the calm feeling the dentist wishes to convey.

Colors evoke specific emotional responses. For example, red can be powerful, exciting, passionate, and daring. Within each color innumerable values or tints, and shades generate an even wider range of response. Red goes from palest romantic pink to a sophisticated deep burgundy. Creating powerful color combinations from numerous hues, tints, and shades is the ultimate objective of working with color.

To develop an accurate response to the language of color, it is first necessary to understand the harmony of color. This means knowing what colors to use and in what order and proportion to create a desired mood, to communicate an idea, or to elicit a reaction.

Color Harmony 2 is the perfect guide for graphic designers, interior designers, fashion designers, architects, marketers, artists, and craftspeople, in fact anyone who wants to understand the language of color. It is a working tool for everyone—the fashion designer faced with color decisions for a new fall line, the interior designer working to create a corporate atmosphere or the young mother selecting yarns for her child's new sweater.

Color Harmony 2 sets guidelines on how to create effective color combinations. It explores feelings and moods with a wide variety of colors and color combination possibilities, with 106 color choices and 1,400 color schemes and combinations based on specific emotional messages. A twelve-segment color wheel provides a foundation for determining unique color solutions. Although the basic schemes and their accompanying companion colors give an infinite range of suggestions, only the human eye can judge the final artistic result.

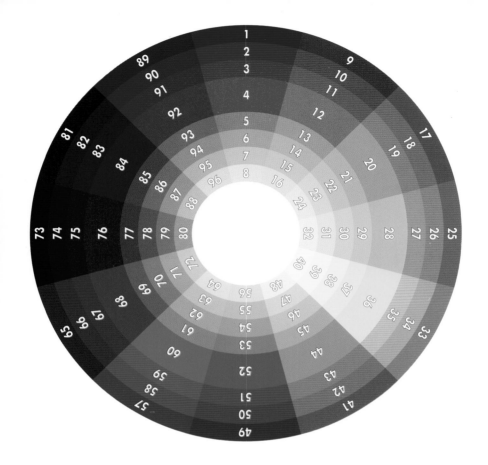

The Color Wheel

The twelve segments of the color wheel consist of primary, secondary, and tertiary hues and their specific tints and shades. With red at the top, the color wheel identifies the three *primary* hues of red, yellow, and blue. These three primary colors form an equilateral triangle within the circle. The three *secondary* hues of orange, violet, and green are located between each primary hue and form

another triangle. Red-orange, yellow-orange, yellow-green, blue-green, blue-violet, and red-violet are the six *tertiary* hues. They result from the combination of a primary and a secondary hue.

Constructed in an orderly progression, the color wheel enables the user to visualize the sequence of color balance and harmony.

8

How to Use Color

Working with color to achieve intended results can be a challenge, but it can also be fun! An effective color scheme can make a room feel warm and inviting, a graphic design able to attract attention, or a poster to recall days gone by. Before learning what colors to use in order to achieve the best results, one must first understand some basic color terms.

Each primary, secondary, and tertiary hue is at a level of full *saturation*, or brightness, which means that there is no black, white, or gray added. Color is described in terms of *value*, which is the lightness or darkness of a color, or the relative amount of white or black in a hue. White added in increments to any of the twelve colors results in lighter values of the hue called *tints*. For example, pink is a tint of the primary color red. The incremental addition of black or gray to a hue results in darker values of the hue known as *shades*. A shade of red is burgundy or maroon. These shades and tints are illustrated by the color chart on the following pages.

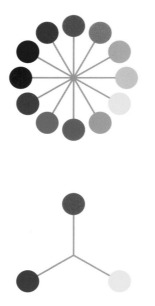

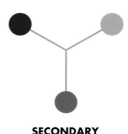

SECONDARY

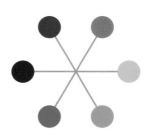

PRIMARY

TERTIARY

The Color Chart

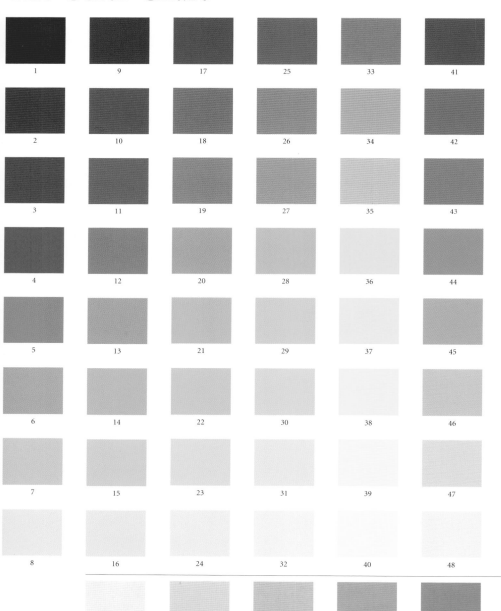

1 9 17 25 33 41
2 10 18 26 34 42
3 11 19 27 35 43
4 12 20 28 36 44
5 13 21 29 37 45
6 14 22 30 38 46
7 15 23 31 39 47
8 16 24 32 40 48

97 98 99 100 101

The color chart is the color wheel in chart form. The rows above and below the fully saturated center hue represent the tints and shades of each color. Each hue, tint, and shade on the chart below is numbered 1–96 for easy reference. Numbers 97–106 represent the value range from lightest gray to black. These numbers correspond with the colors used in combination throughout the book and offer a wide selection of balanced and effective color possibilities within each interpretive section.

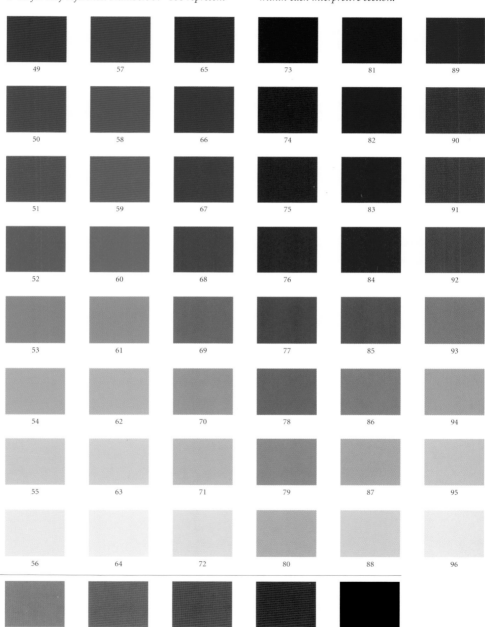

The Process

Color Harmony 2 is divided into sections to show aspects of color and color combinations that visually explain the effect color has on our lives. The color conversion chart and the color wheel, on pages 8–11, and color cards all work together to develop unique color possibilities. Color Harmony 2 explores color terminology, the aspects of color, color schemes, and color combinations. It serves as a practical guide for accurate and positive results when designing with color.

STEP 1

Clearly define the results you want to achieve with color.

STEP 2

Select a main color that reflects the needs of the project.

STEP 3

Select a color scheme based on the choice of the central hue.

STEP 4

Refine the available color choices in terms of the particular project or individual sensibility.

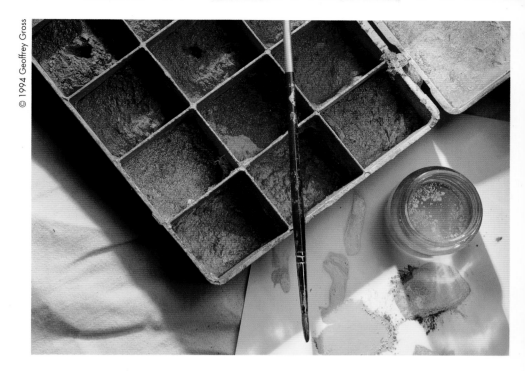

Aspects of Color

The aspects, or qualities of color, refer to colors and color combinations that evoke certain emotional responses. We use many words to describe the properties of individual colors and to compare and contrast them, but *light* and *dark* is the basic distinction. Without sunlight or artificial light, there is no color. We depend on light for color, which we use in countless combinations to express our ideas and emotions.

The following aspects of color contain color combinations that exist in harmony with each other, and are in spectral balance. *Spectral balance* occurs within the eye as thousands of waves of electromagnetic energy of different lengths bounce off (or are absorbed by) the chemical components of any object. Light waves reflect red, yellow, and blue, and the rods and cones in the eye's retina simultaneously mix and sort these reflected colors into thousands of tints and shades, which work to offer endless possibilities for specific color use.

Color is both simple and complex. It means different things to different people in different cultures. No color is seen the same way by any two people. Color is personal and universal, sending messages full of endless variations.

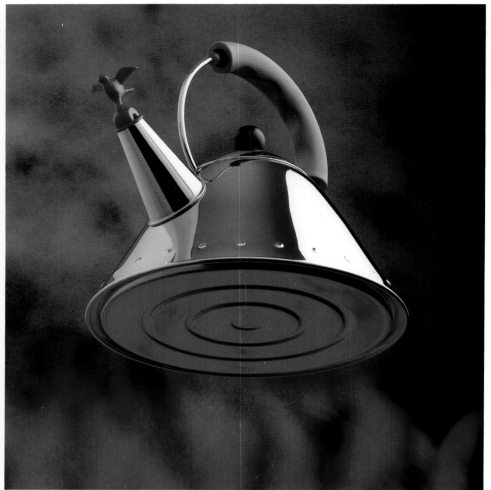

Hot

Hot refers to red in full saturation on the color wheel; this is red at its strongest.

Hot colors project outward and attract attention. For this reason, red is often used in graphic signage and design.

Hot colors are strong and aggressive and seem to vibrate within their own space. The power of hot colors affects people in many ways, such as increasing blood pressure and stimulating the nervous system.

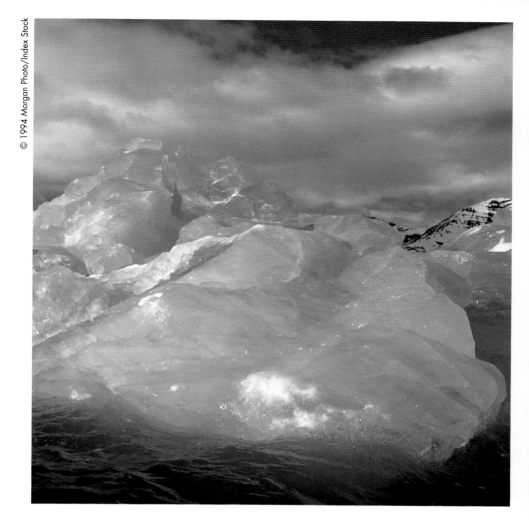

Cold

Cold refers to fully saturated blue. At its brightest it is dominating and strong.

Cold colors remind one of ice and snow. The feelings generated by cold colors—blue, green, and blue-green— are the direct opposite of those generated by hot colors; cold blue slows the metabolism and increases one's sense of calm. When placed next to each other, cold and hot colors vibrate like fire and ice.

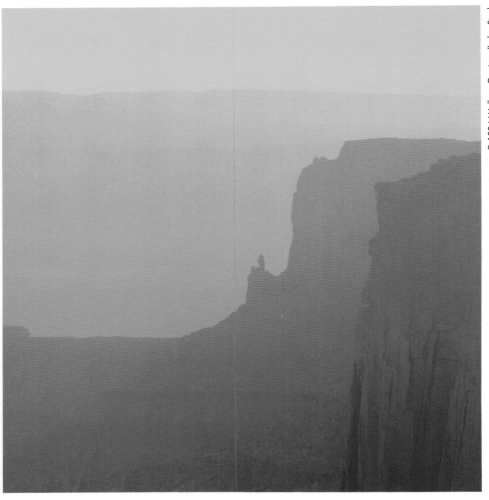

Warm

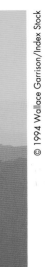

All hues that contain red are warm. It is the addition of yellow to red that makes warm colors substantially different from hot colors. Warm colors, such as red-orange, orange, and yellow-orange, always contain a mixture of red and yellow in their composition and encompass a larger part of the emotional spectrum.

Warm colors are comforting, spontaneous, and welcoming. Like an Arizona sunset, the warmth of these hues radiates outward and surrounds everything in reach.

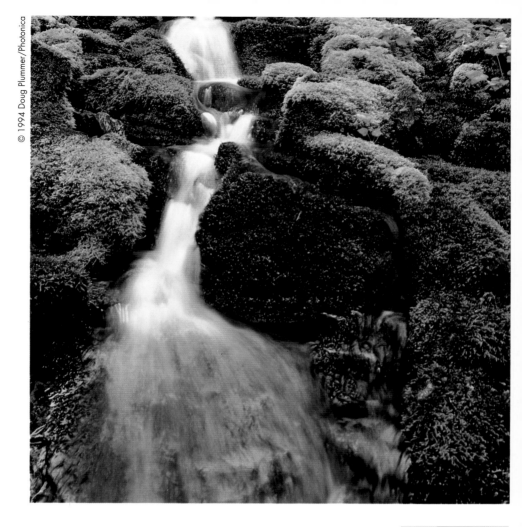

Cool

Cool colors are based in blue. They differ from cold colors because of the addition of yellow to their composition, which creates yellow-green, green, and blue-green. Cool colors, such as turquoise blue and verdant green, are seen in nature. Like spring growth, they make us feel renewed. Soothing and calm, these hues provide a sense of depth as well as comfort. Cool colors are like a swim in a refreshing, tropical pool.

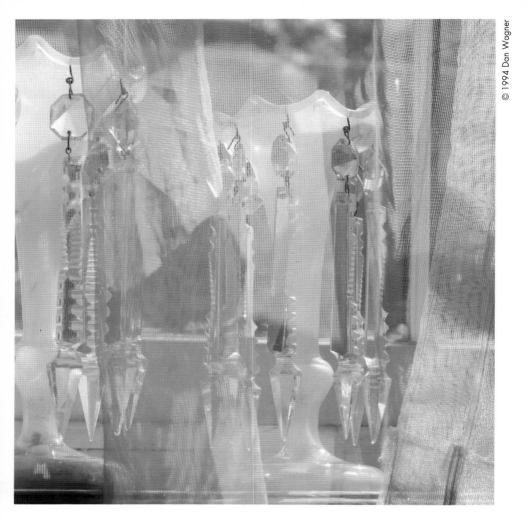

Light

Light colors are the palest pastels. They take their lightness from an absence of visible color in their composition, and are almost transparent. When lightness increases, variations between the different hues decrease.

Light colors open up the surroundings and suggest airiness, rest, and liquidity. They resemble sheer curtains at a window and send a message of relaxation.

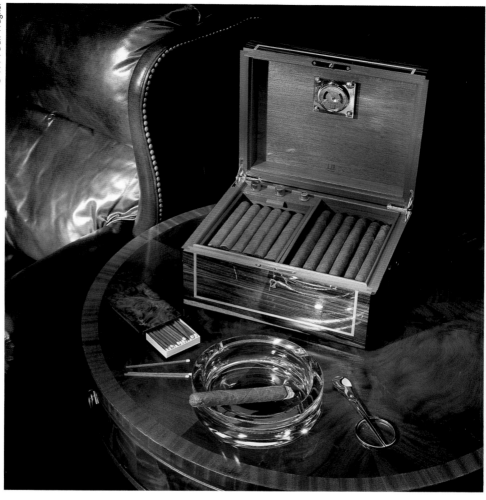

Dark

Dark colors are hues that contain black in their composition. They close up space and make it seem smaller. Dark colors are concentrated and serious in their effect. Seasonally, they suggest autumn and winter. Combining lights and darks together is a common and dramatic way to represent the opposites in nature, such as night and day.

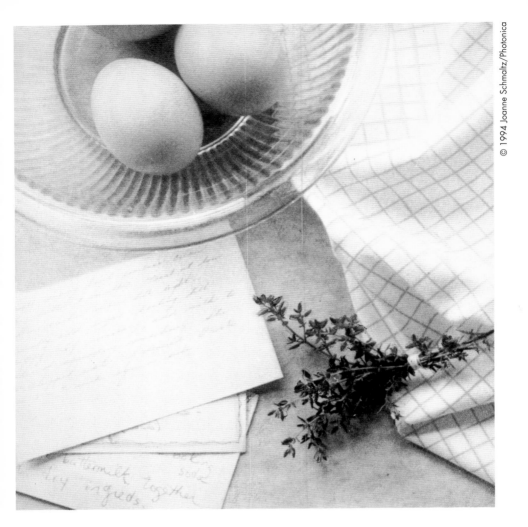

Pale

Pale hues are the softest pastels. They contain at least 65 percent white in their composition, and have a diminished hue which is most often referred to as soft or romantic.

Pale colors, like ivory, light blue, and pink, suggest gentleness. They can be seen in the clouds in a soft, early light, or in the lavender colors of a misty morning. Because they are calming colors, pale hues are frequently used in interior spaces.

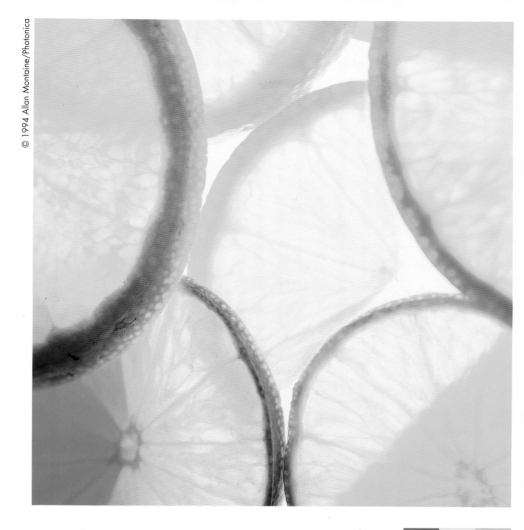

Bright

The amount of pure color within a hue determines its brightness. The clarity of bright colors is achieved by the omission of gray or black. Blues, reds, yellows, and oranges are colors in full brightness.

Bright colors are vivid and attract attention. A yellow school bus, a bunch of colored balloons, the red of a clown's nose, never go unnoticed. Exhilarating and cheerful, bright colors are perfect for use in packaging, fashion, and advertising.

Basic Color Schemes

No color stands alone. In fact, the effect of a color is determined by many factors: the light reflected from it, the colors that surround it, or the perspective of the person looking at the color.

There are ten basic color schemes. They are called achromatic, analogous, clash, complement, monochromatic, neutral, and split complement, as well as primary, secondary, and tertiary schemes.

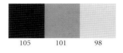

105   101   98

ACHROMATIC SCHEME

Without color, uses only black, white, and grays.

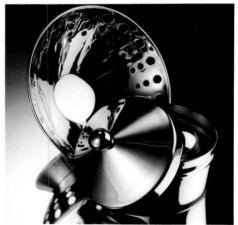

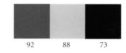

92   88   73

ANALOGOUS SCHEME

Uses any three consecutive hues or any of their tints and shades on the color wheel.

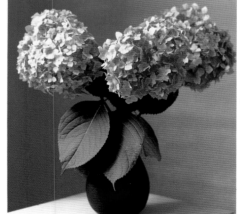

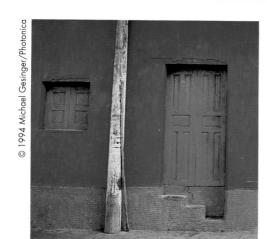

4   68

CLASH SCHEME

Combines a color with the hue to the right or left of its complement on the color wheel.

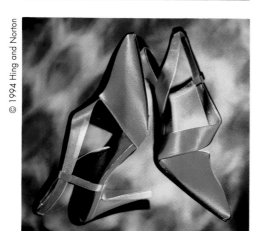

92   44

COMPLEMENTARY SCHEME

Uses direct opposites on the color wheel.

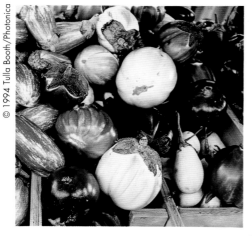

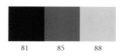

81   85   88

MONOCHROMATIC SCHEME

Uses one hue in combination with any or all of its tints and shades.

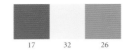

17 32 26

NEUTRAL SCHEME

Uses a hue which has been diminished or neutralized by the addition of its complement or black.

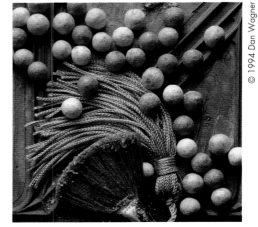

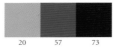

20 57 73

SPLIT COMPLEMENTARY SCHEME

Consists of a hue and the two hues on either side of its complement.

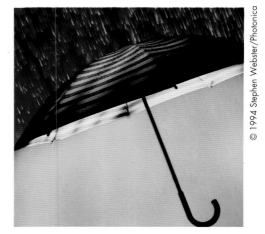

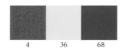

4 36 68

PRIMARY SCHEME

A combination of the pure hues of red, yellow, and blue.

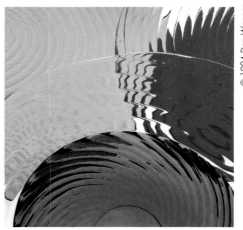

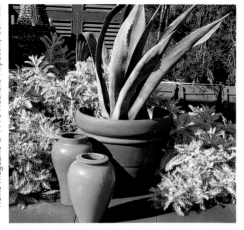

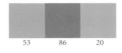

53　　86　　20

SECONDARY SCHEME

A combination of the secondary hues of green, violet, and orange.

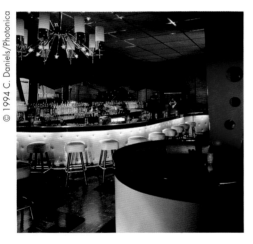

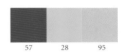

57　　28　　95

TERTIARY TRIAD SCHEME

A tertiary triad is one of two combinations: red-orange, yellow-green, and blue-violet, or blue-green, yellow-orange, and red-violet; all of which are equidistant from each other on the color wheel.

COLOR COMBINATIONS FOR CREATIVE EFFECTS

The color schemes and combinations on the following pages illustrate over 1,400 color possibilities. Creative color solutions are presented with practical and emotional variations providing a wide range of color uses in all areas of the fine, graphic, and applied arts.

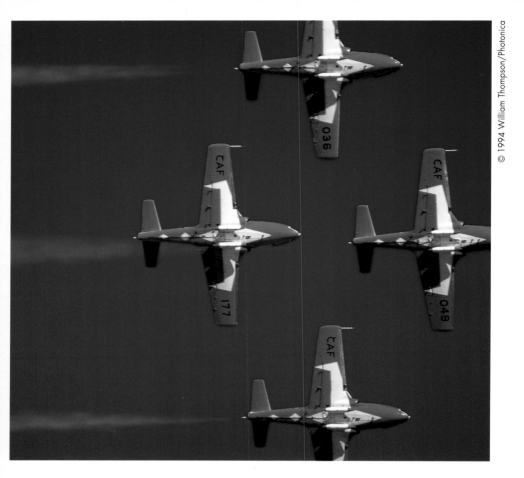

Powerful

The most powerful combinations, full of excitement and control, are always associated with the color red. No matter what color it is combined with, red can never be ignored. It is the ultimate "power" color—forceful, bold, and extreme. Powerful color combinations are symbols of our strongest emotions, love and hate. They represent emotional overdrive.

In advertising and display, powerful color combinations are used to send a strong message of vitality and awareness. They always attract attention.

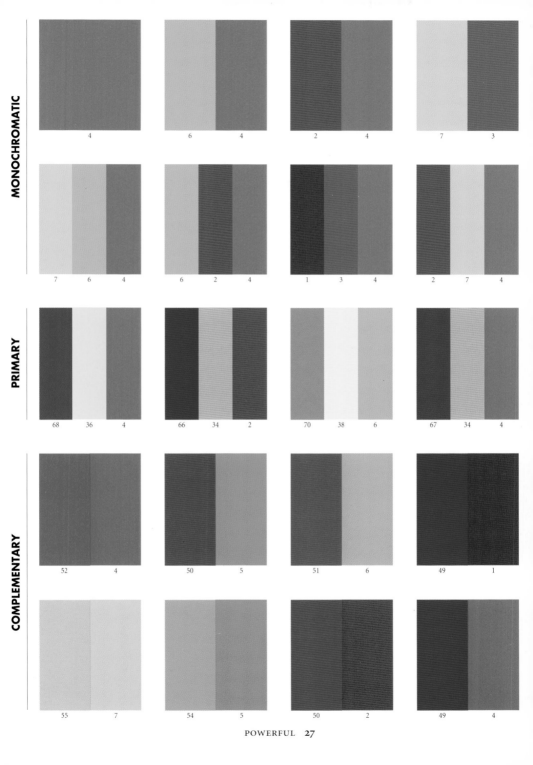

| 84 | 92 | 4 | | 84 | 94 | 4 | | 87 | 93 | 4 | | 86 | 94 | 3 |

| 92 | 4 | 12 | | 92 | 5 | 12 | | 95 | 6 | 12 | | 94 | 2 | 14 |

| 4 | 12 | 20 | | 3 | 13 | 20 | | 6 | 16 | 20 | | 7 | 11 | 22 |

| 44 | 4 | 60 | | 41 | 4 | 62 | | 47 | 4 | 63 | | 46 | 2 | 60 |

| 1 | 44 | 60 | | 7 | 45 | 59 | | 2 | 44 | 57 | | 5 | 44 | 61 |

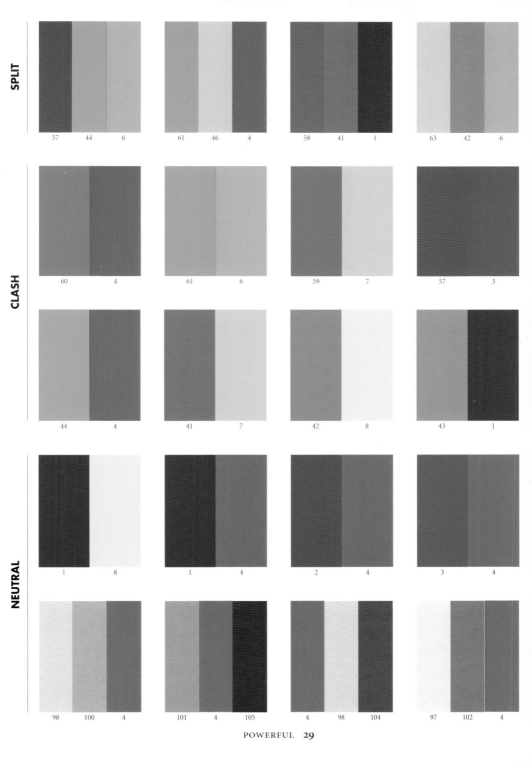

57   44   6

61   46   4

58   41   1

63   42   6

60   4

61   6

59   7

57   3

44   4

41   7

42   8

43   1

1   8

1   4

2   4

3   4

98   100   4

101   4   105

4   98   104

97   102   4

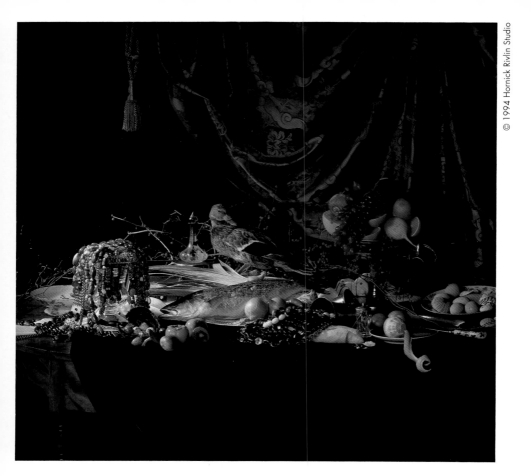

Rich

Richness in a color can be created by combining a powerful hue with its darkened complement. For example, deep burgundy results from adding black to red, and, like a fine old wine from a French vineyard, it signifies wealth. Burgundy and deep forest green used together with gold suggest affluence. These dark, sumptuous colors—used in textures as diverse as leather and taffeta—create a dramatic, unforgettable effect. They will always reveal a sense of wealth and status.

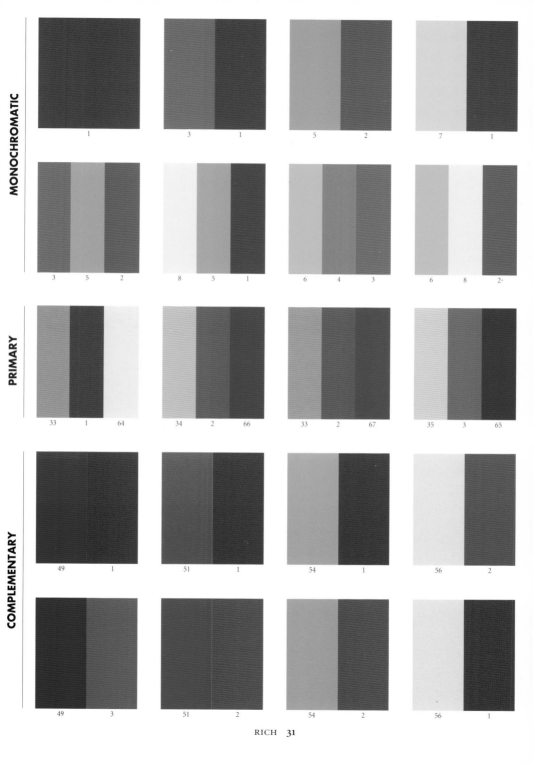

PRIMARY

COMPLEMENTARY

| 81 | 89 | 1 | | 82 | 91 | 2 | | 84 | 90 | 3 | | 88 | 92 | 1 |

| 89 | 1 | 9 | | 90 | 2 | 11 | | 94 | 2 | 10 | | 3 | 95 | 10 |

| 1 | 9 | 17 | | 2 | 11 | 17 | | 3 | 10 | 19 | | 1 | 19 | 9 |

| 57 | 1 | 41 | | 58 | 1 | 42 | | 62 | 1 | 46 | | 64 | 1 | 45 |

| 61 | 2 | 42 | | 58 | 2 | 43 | | 60 | 3 | 41 | | 63 | 3 | 45 |

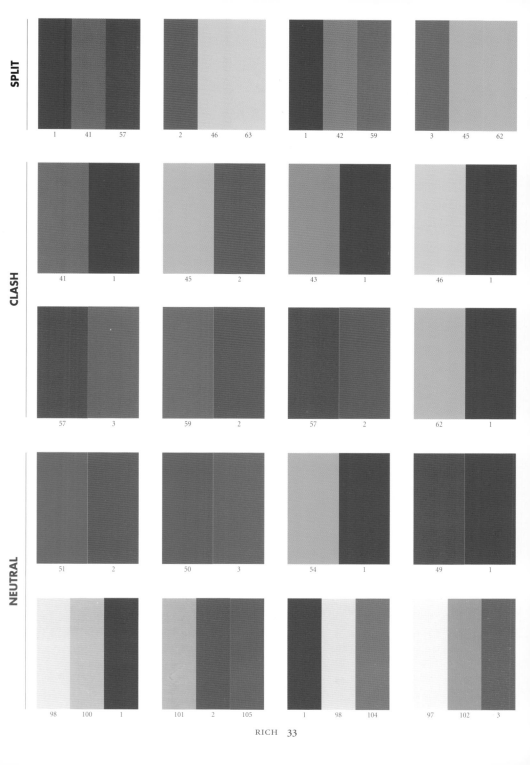

SPLIT

| 1 | 41 | 57 | 2 | 46 | 63 | 1 | 42 | 59 | 3 | 45 | 62 |

CLASH

| 41 | 1 | 45 | 2 | 43 | 1 | 46 | 1 |

| 57 | 3 | 59 | 2 | 57 | 2 | 62 | 1 |

NEUTRAL

| 51 | 2 | 50 | 3 | 54 | 1 | 49 | 1 |

| 98 | 100 | 1 | 101 | 2 | 105 | 1 | 98 | 104 | 97 | 102 | 3 |

RICH 33

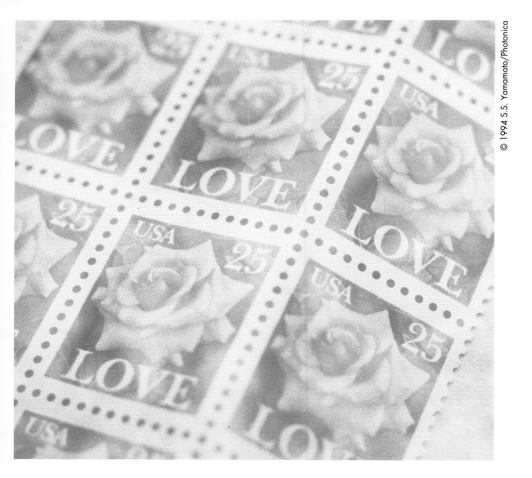

Romantic

Pink suggests romance. Pink is white added to red in varying amounts and is the lightened value of red. Like red, pink arouses interest and excitement, but in a softer, quieter way.

A romantic color scheme using pastel tints of pink, lavender, and peach will read as gentle and tender. Combined with other bright pastels, pink evokes memories of dreamy June days and full bouquets of delicate, summer flowers.

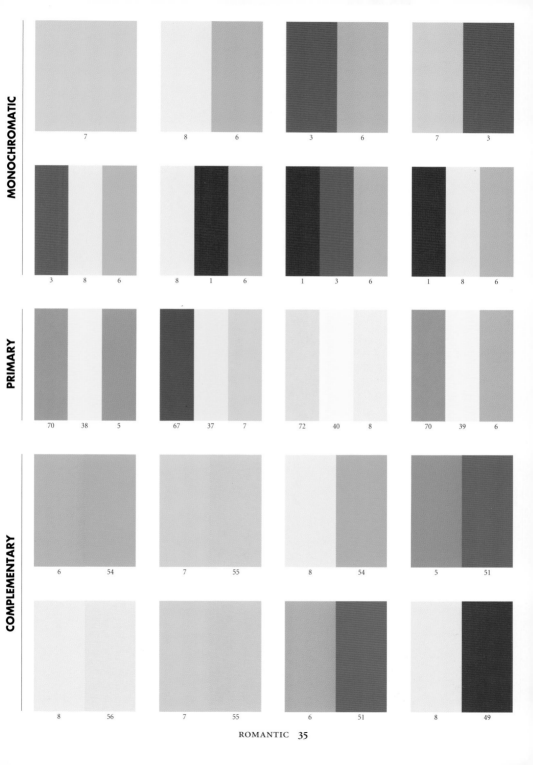

| 86 | 94 | 6 | | 87 | 95 | 7 | | 87 | 96 | 8 | | 87 | 94 | 6 |

| 94 | 6 | 15 | | 95 | 7 | 14 | | 93 | 7 | 16 | | 96 | 5 | 15 |

| 6 | 14 | 22 | | 5 | 16 | 23 | | 7 | 16 | 22 | | 8 | 12 | 23 |

| 46 | 6 | 62 | | 45 | 6 | 63 | | 47 | 7 | 63 | | 46 | 3 | 64 |

| 44 | 8 | 61 | | 47 | 7 | 59 | | 43 | 6 | 57 | | 47 | 6 | 60 |

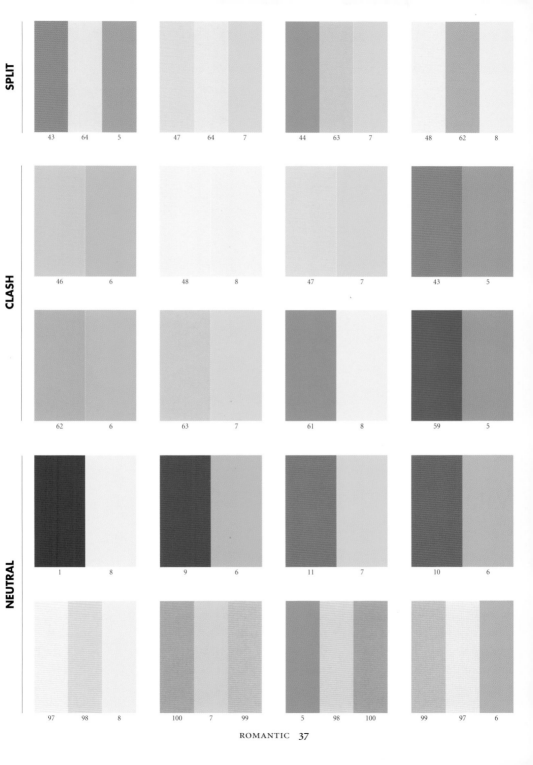

SPLIT

| 43 | 64 | 5 | | 47 | 64 | 7 | | 44 | 63 | 7 | | 48 | 62 | 8 |

CLASH

| 46 | 6 | | 48 | 8 | | 47 | 7 | | 43 | 5 |

| 62 | 6 | | 63 | 7 | | 61 | 8 | | 59 | 5 |

NEUTRAL

| 1 | 8 | | 9 | 6 | | 11 | 7 | | 10 | 6 |

| 97 | 98 | 8 | | 100 | 7 | 99 | | 5 | 98 | 100 | | 99 | 97 | 6 |

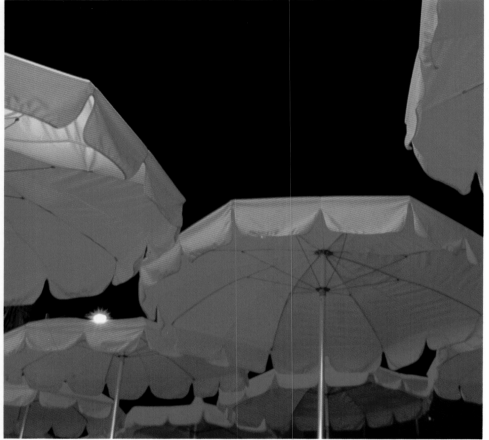

Vital

Vitality and enthusiasm are best promoted in design and graphics by using the hue most commonly known as vermillion, or any of its many tints and shades. By using color combinations with this red-orange hue at the center, a feeling of vigor and warmth can easily be created. These combinations are youthful and playful and are often seen in advertisements displaying energetic lifestyles and personalities. The combination of red-orange partnered with its complement, turquoise, is active, easy to be around, and is very effective when used in fabrics, advertising, and packaging.

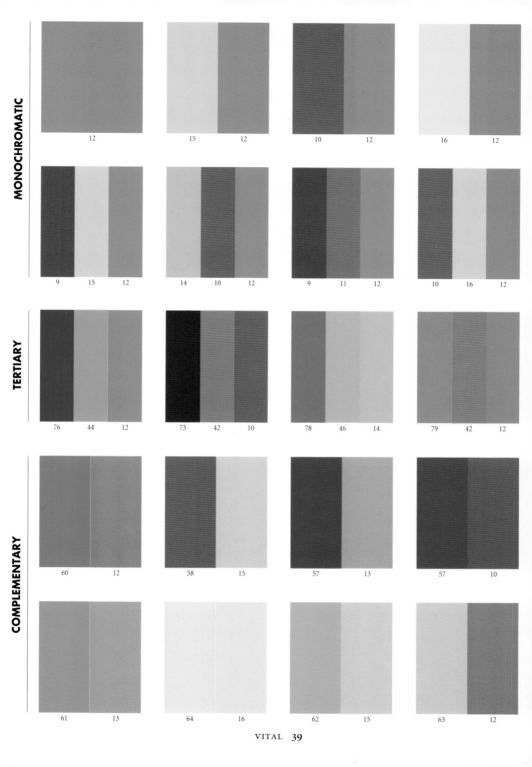

MONOCHROMATIC

12

15 12

10 12

16 12

9 15 12

14 10 12

9 11 12

10 16 12

TERTIARY

76 44 12

73 42 10

78 46 14

79 42 12

COMPLEMENTARY

60 12

58 15

57 13

57 10

61 13

64 16

62 15

63 12

92	4	12
90	6	13
93	5	12
94	5	11

4	12	20
4	15	20
7	13	20
8	10	22

12	20	28
11	23	28
15	24	28
14	18	32

52	12	68
50	12	70
54	12	71
55	10	68

9	68	52
13	70	51
11	68	50
14	68	55

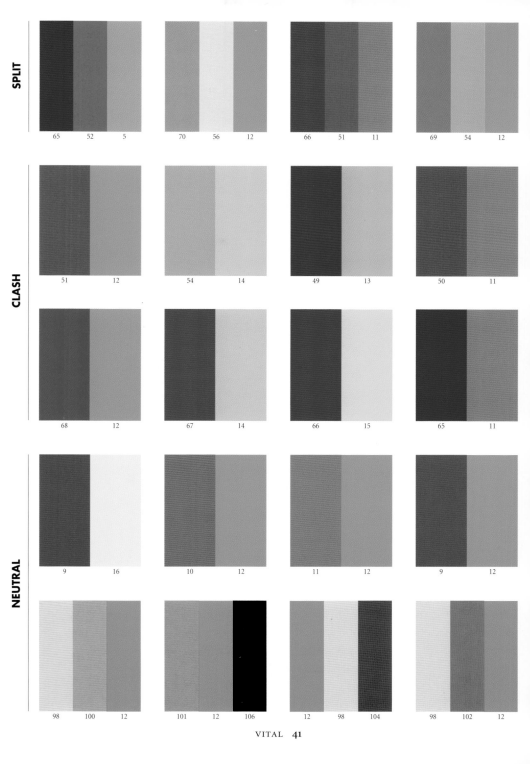

SPLIT

65	52	5
70	56	12
66	51	11
69	54	12

CLASH

51	12
54	14
49	13
50	11

68	12
67	14
66	15
65	11

NEUTRAL

9	16
10	12
11	12
9	12

98	100	12
101	12	106
12	98	104
98	102	12

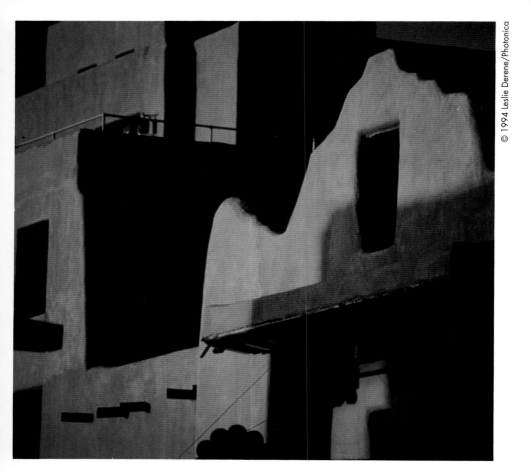

Earthy

Rich, warm, and full of vitality, earthy color combinations frequently use the dark, vivid red-orange called terra-cotta. Terra-cotta suggests subtle warmth, like polished copper. When used with white, it projects a brilliant, natural combination.

Earthy hues reflect fun-loving youth, and call to mind leisure living. As part of an analogous scheme, these warm, earthy tones generate exciting combinations, such as those seen in the decor of the American West.

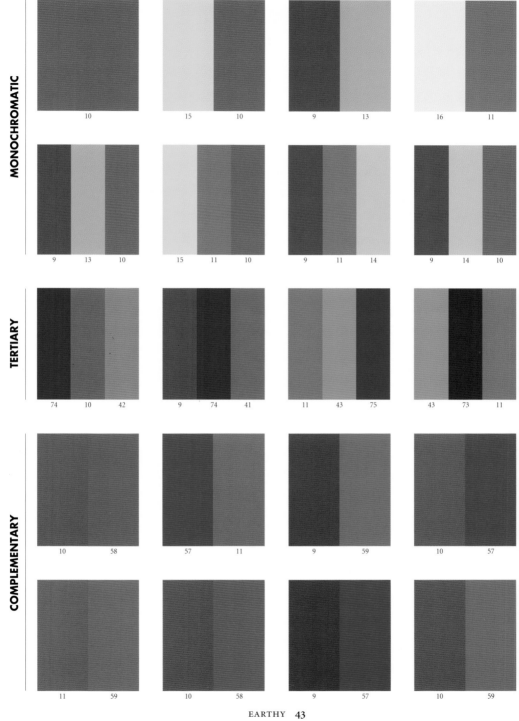

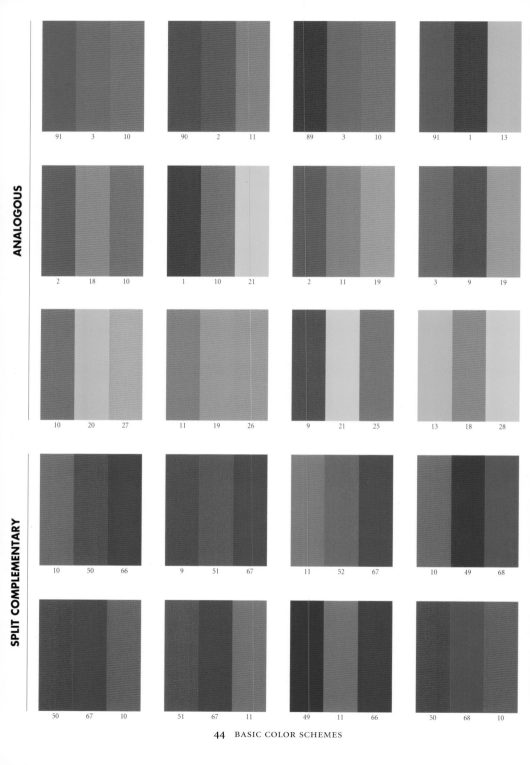

91	3	10

90	2	11

89	3	10

91	1	13

2	18	10

1	10	21

2	11	19

3	9	19

10	20	27

11	19	26

9	21	25

13	18	28

10	50	66

9	51	67

11	52	67

10	49	68

50	67	10

51	67	11

49	11	66

50	68	10

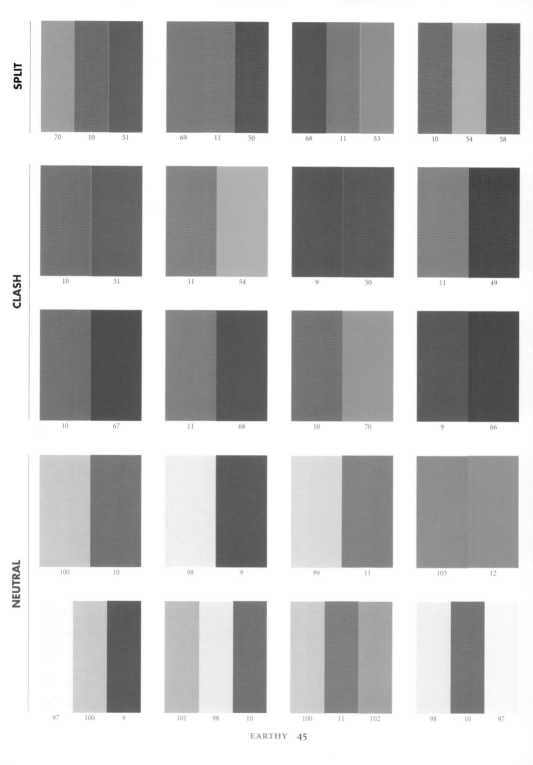

SPLIT

70 10 51 69 11 50 68 11 53 10 54 58

CLASH

10 51 11 54 9 50 11 49

10 67 11 68 10 70 9 66

NEUTRAL

100 10 98 9 99 11 103 12

97 100 9 101 98 10 100 11 102 98 10 97

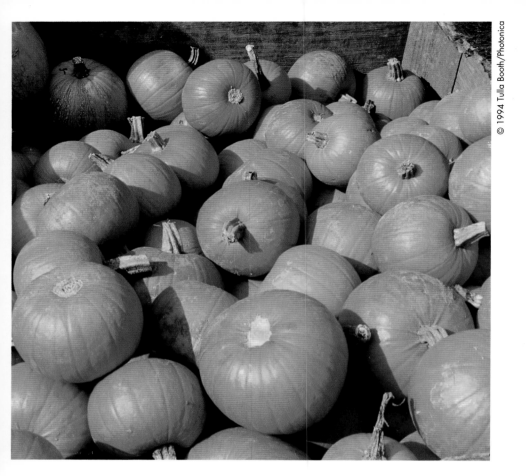

Friendly

Color schemes that convey friendliness often include orange. Open and easy, these combinations have all the elements of energy and movement. They create order and equality without a sense of power or control.

Orange along with its color wheel neighbors is frequently used in fast-food restaurants because it projects an inviting message of good food at a friendly price. Because it is energetic and glowing, orange is the international safety color in areas of danger. Orange life rafts and life preservers are easily seen on blue or gray seas.

MONOCHROMATIC

20

23 | 20

17 | 20

24 | 18

19 | 22 | 20

23 | 18 | 20

17 | 19 | 20

18 | 23 | 20

SECONDARY

84 | 20 | 52

81 | 17 | 50

86 | 21 | 53

84 | 18 | 52

COMPLEMENTARY

68 | 20

67 | 23

66 | 21

65 | 18

70 | 22

72 | 21

67 | 19

65 | 20

4	12	20
4	14	20
7	16	20
6	15	18

12	20	27
12	22	26
14	24	26
15	18	20

20	28	36
19	29	36
22	32	36
21	27	38

76	20	60
74	20	62
78	20	63
79	19	60

18	76	60
22	79	58
19	76	59
21	76	61

48   BASIC COLOR SCHEMES

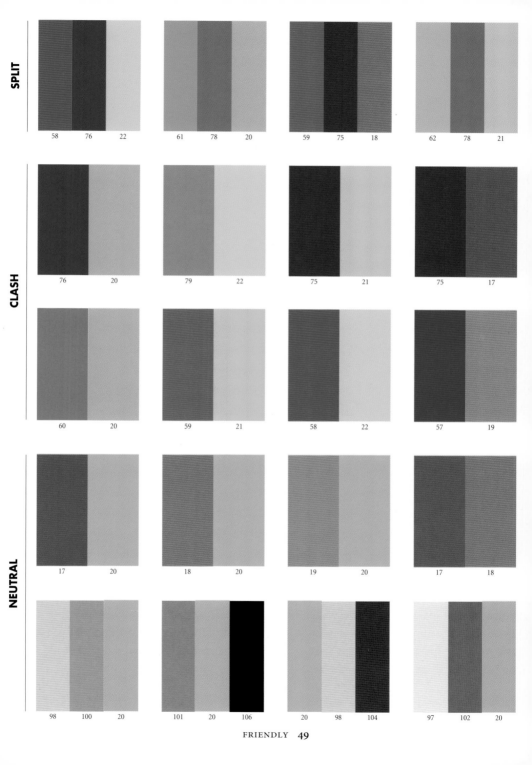

SPLIT

58 76 22   61 78 20   59 75 18   62 78 21

CLASH

76 20   79 22   75 21   75 17

60 20   59 21   58 22   57 19

NEUTRAL

17 20   18 20   19 20   17 18

98 100 20   101 20 106   20 98 104   97 102 20

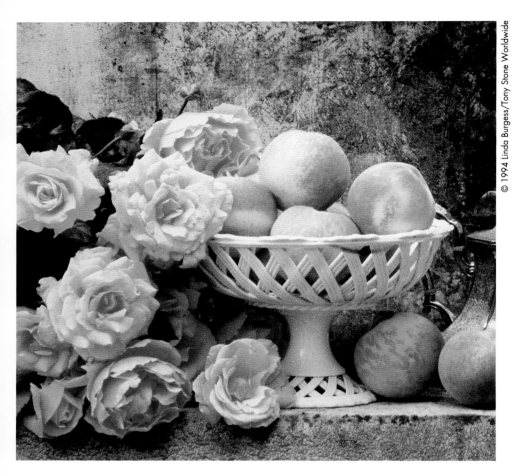

Soft

Light-valued tints without high contrast are the most comfortable to use when creating soft color combinations. Peach, as part of a muted palette, is delicious and appealing in its color message and workable in any setting, from restaurants to store displays to fashion. When combined with tints of violet and green, it becomes part of a subdued but magical secondary color scheme.

These soft and relaxing colors are often ideal for home decor. The combinations are cheerful and outgoing, while at the same time calm and inviting.

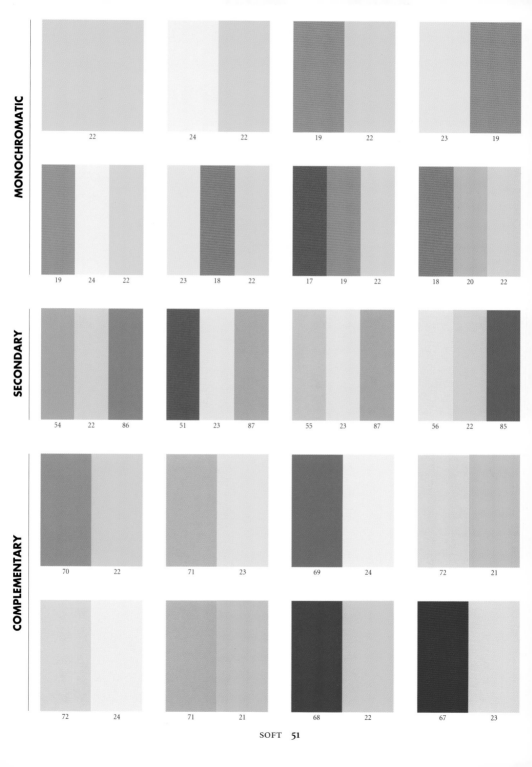

22

24   22

19   22

23   19

19   24   22

23   18   22

17   19   22

18   20   22

54   22   86

51   23   87

55   23   87

56   22   85

70   22

71   23

69   24

72   21

72   24

71   21

68   22

67   23

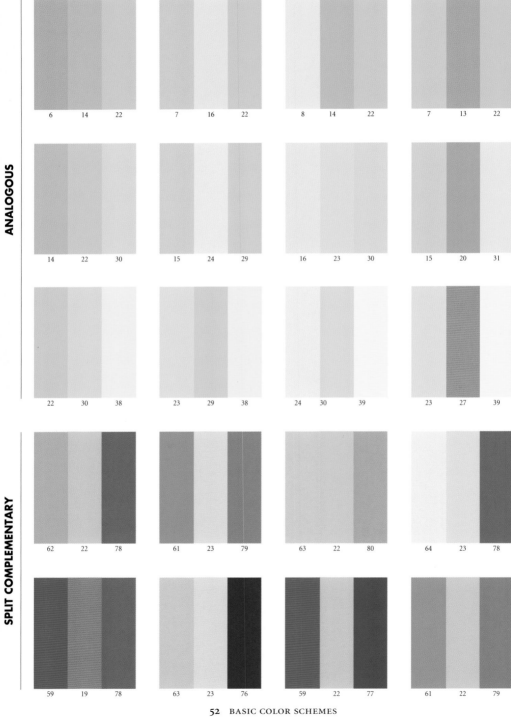

ANALOGOUS

| 6 | 14 | 22 | | 7 | 16 | 22 | | 8 | 14 | 22 | | 7 | 13 | 22 |

| 14 | 22 | 30 | | 15 | 24 | 29 | | 16 | 23 | 30 | | 15 | 20 | 31 |

| 22 | 30 | 38 | | 23 | 29 | 38 | | 24 | 30 | 39 | | 23 | 27 | 39 |

SPLIT COMPLEMENTARY

| 62 | 22 | 78 | | 61 | 23 | 79 | | 63 | 22 | 80 | | 64 | 23 | 78 |

| 59 | 19 | 78 | | 63 | 23 | 76 | | 59 | 22 | 77 | | 61 | 22 | 79 |

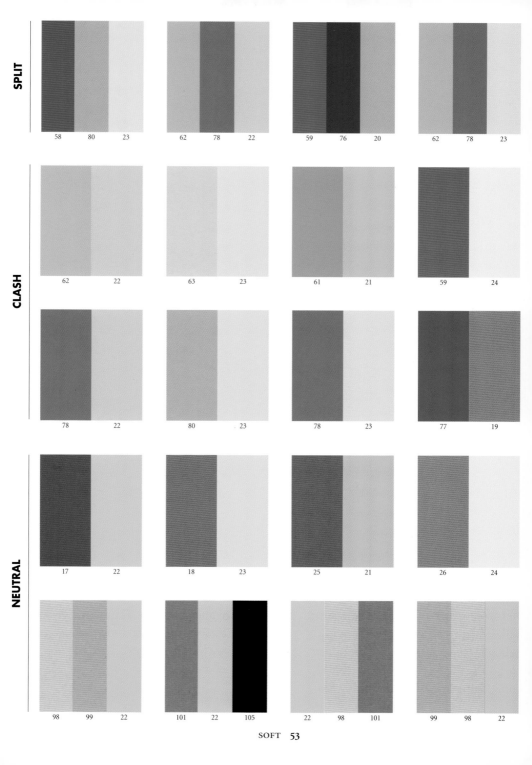

SPLIT

58	80	23
62	78	22
59	76	20
62	78	23

CLASH

62	22
63	23
61	21
59	24

78	22
80	23
78	23
77	19

NEUTRAL

17	22
18	23
25	21
26	24

98	99	22
101	22	105
22	98	101
99	98	22

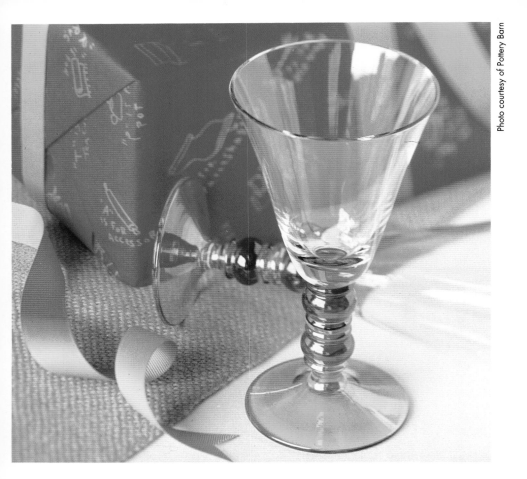

Welcoming

Color combinations using yellow-orange or amber are the most welcoming. Yellow combined with a small amount of red creates these radiant hues which are universally appealing. In full strength, yellow-orange or amber can be likened to gold or the precious spice saffron. A monochromatic color scheme of saffron used with white is one of classic beauty and is very inviting.

Combinations made with pale amber are warm and congenial. This hue can be used in a variety of applications that call for creamy tints to express festive and cordial environments.

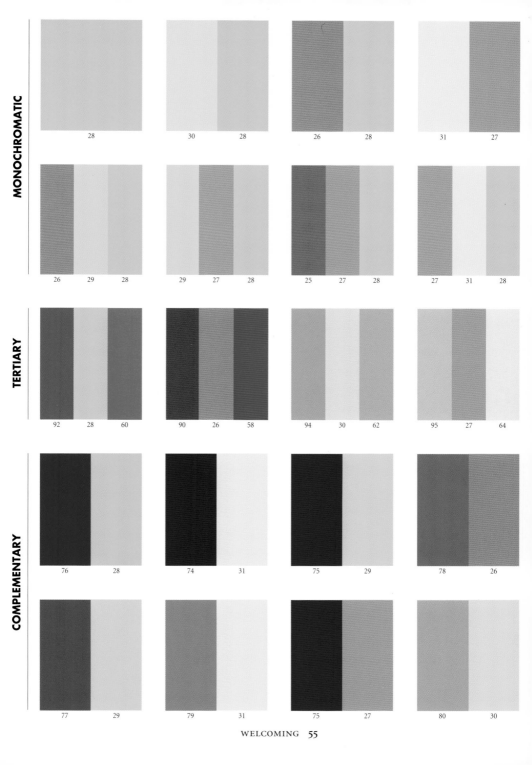

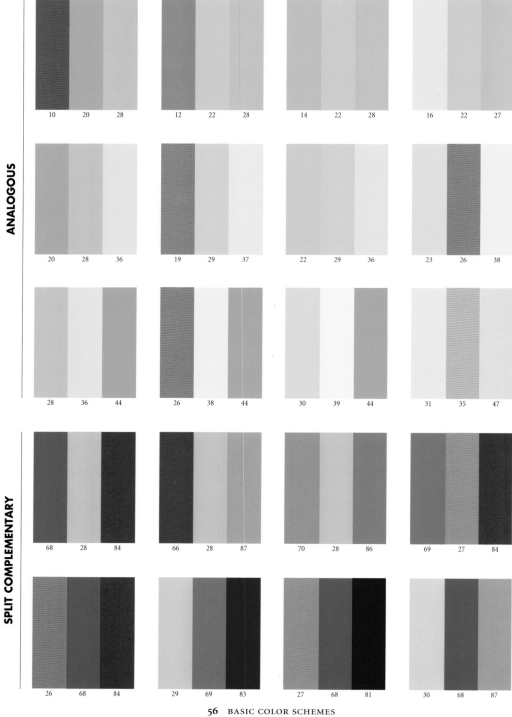

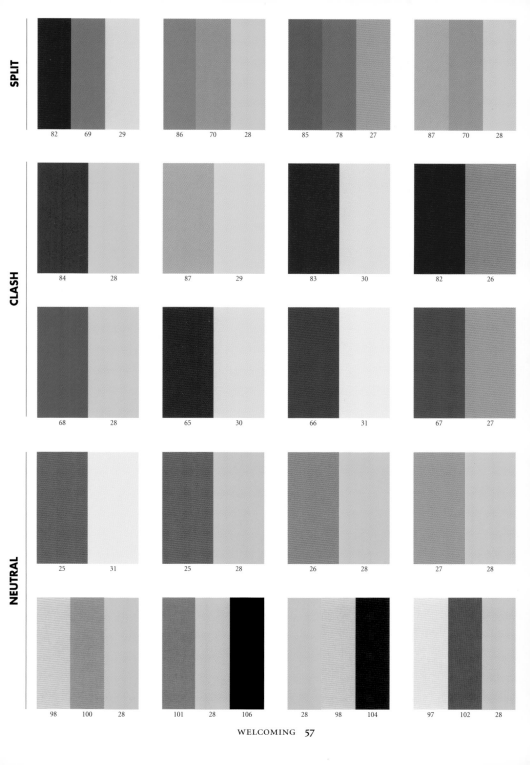

SPLIT

| 82 | 69 | 29 | | 86 | 70 | 28 | | 85 | 78 | 27 | | 87 | 70 | 28 |

CLASH

| 84 | 28 | | 87 | 29 | | 83 | 30 | | 82 | 26 |

| 68 | 28 | | 65 | 30 | | 66 | 31 | | 67 | 27 |

NEUTRAL

| 25 | 31 | | 25 | 28 | | 26 | 28 | | 27 | 28 |

| 98 | 100 | 28 | | 101 | 28 | 106 | | 28 | 98 | 104 | | 97 | 102 | 28 |

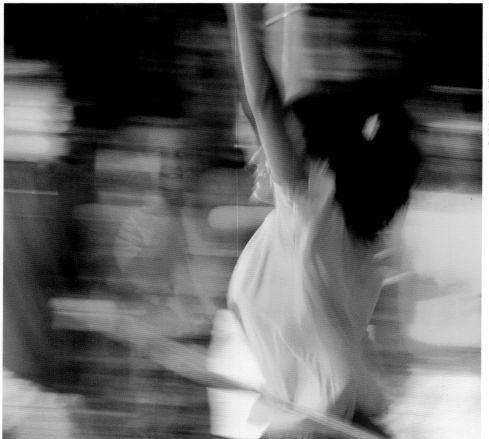

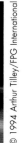

Moving

The brightest color combinations are those that have primary yellow at the center. Yellow expresses life-giving sun, activity, and constant motion. When white is added to yellow, its luminous quality increases and the overall effect is one of extraordinary brightness.

Color schemes of high contrast, such as yellow with its complement violet, mean activity and motion. These palettes generate movement, especially within a round space. It is almost impossible to feel despondent when surrounded by a combination using yellow or any of its tints.

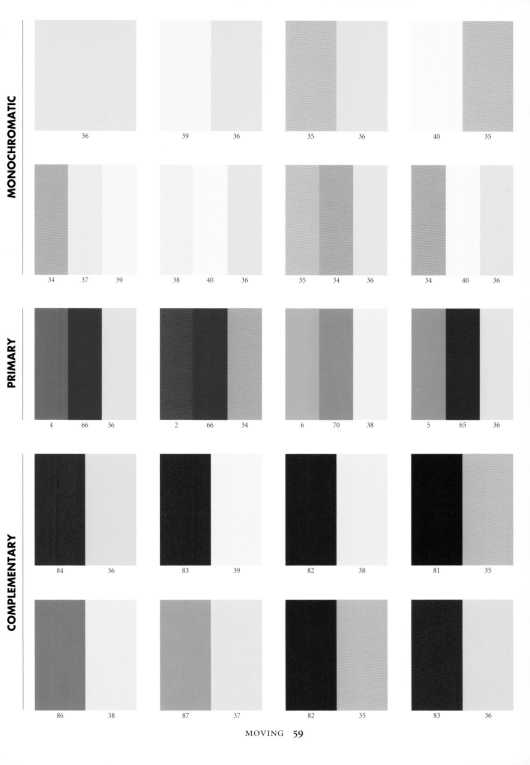

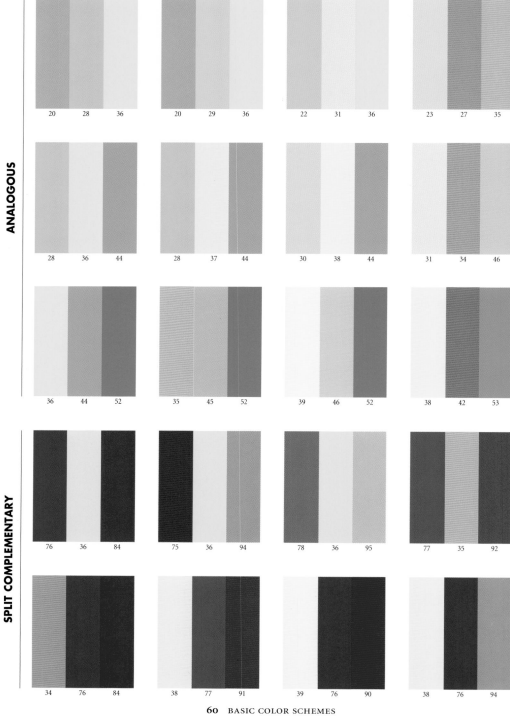

ANALOGOUS

20	28	36
20	29	36
22	31	36
23	27	35
28	36	44
28	37	44
30	38	44
31	34	46
36	44	52
35	45	52
39	46	52
38	42	53

SPLIT COMPLEMENTARY

76	36	84
75	36	94
78	36	95
77	35	92
34	76	84
38	77	91
39	76	90
38	76	94

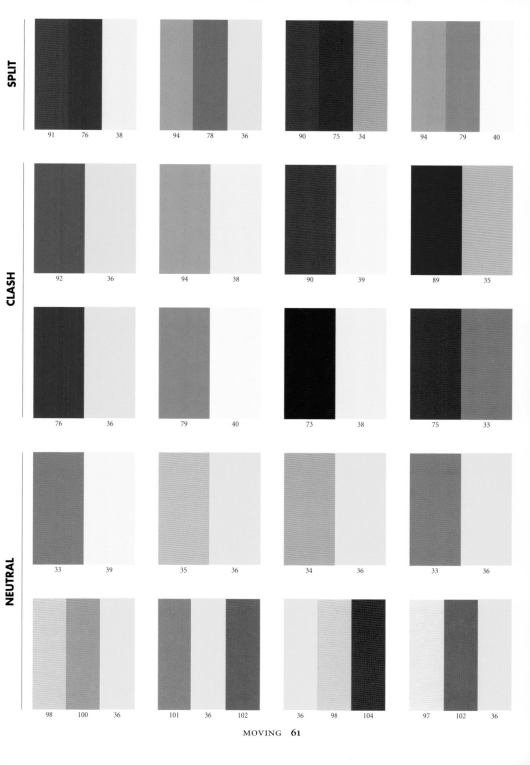

SPLIT

| 91 | 76 | 38 | | 94 | 78 | 36 | | 90 | 75 | 34 | | 94 | 79 | 40 |

CLASH

| 92 | 36 | | 94 | 38 | | 90 | 39 | | 89 | 35 |

| 76 | 36 | | 79 | 40 | | 73 | 38 | | 75 | 33 |

NEUTRAL

| 33 | 39 | | 35 | 36 | | 34 | 36 | | 33 | 36 |

| 98 | 100 | 36 | | 101 | 36 | 102 | | 36 | 98 | 104 | | 97 | 102 | 36 |

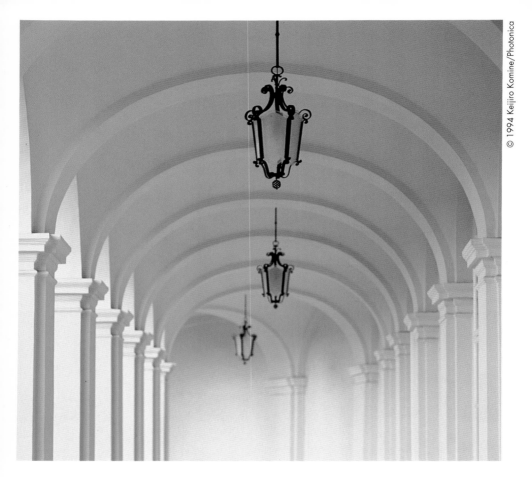

Elegant

Elegant color combinations use only the palest tints. For example, a whisper of yellow combined with white makes a pastel cream, which can be used to create a warmer version of an all-white room. The presence of natural light produces subtle shadows and highlights architectural details, which help to fashion an elegant setting.

Palettes that combine hues similar to the color of eggshells and linens are compatible with most other hues and offer a workable alternative to achromatic white or noncolor schemes. In fashion, elegant linens, silks, wools, and velvets in creamy tones give the impression of ease and opulence by creating a look of classic understatement.

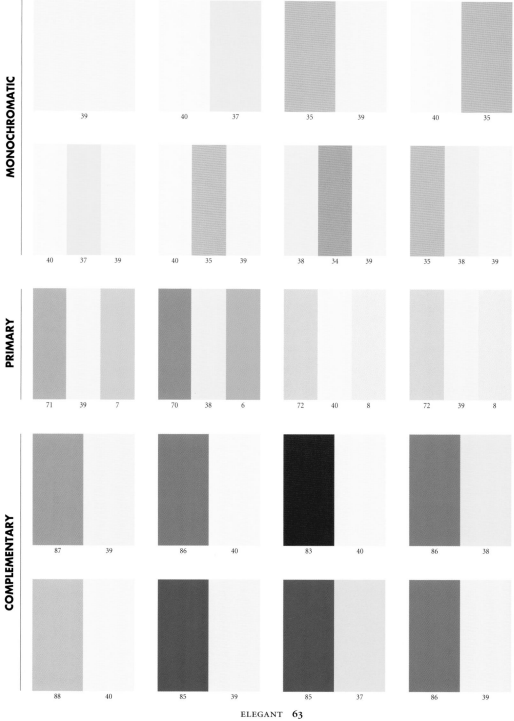

39

40   37

35   39

40   35

40   37   39

40   35   39

38   34   39

35   38   39

71   39   7

70   38   6

72   40   8

72   39   8

87   39

86   40

83   40

86   38

88   40

85   39

85   37

86   39

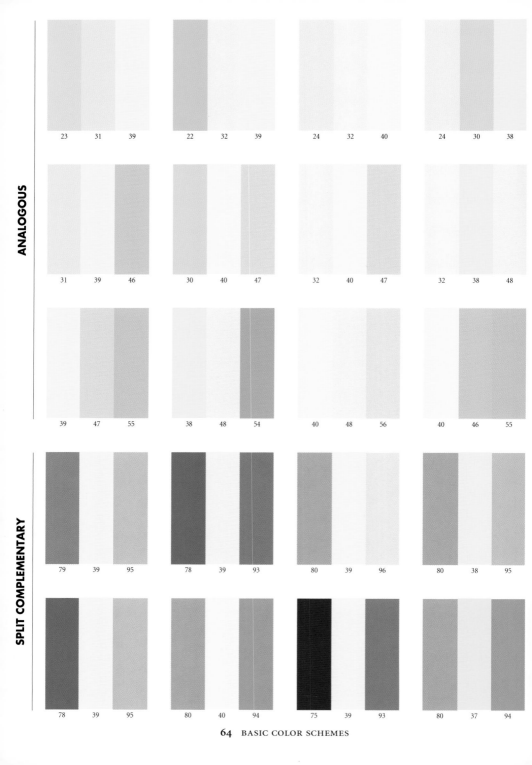

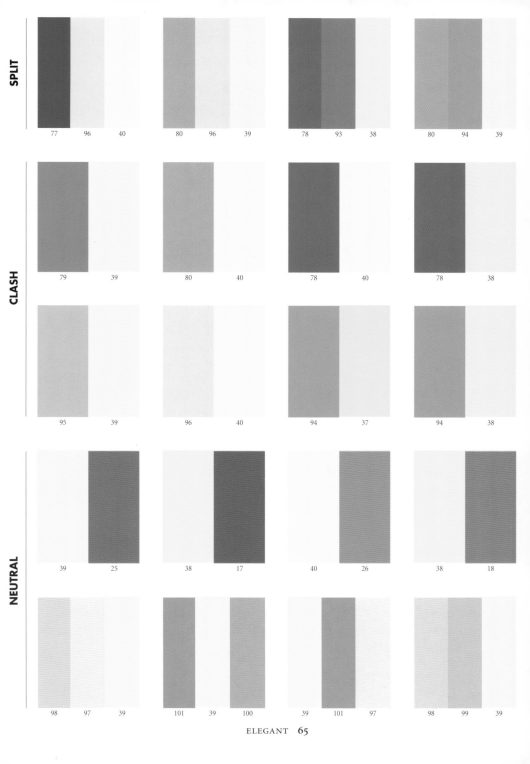

SPLIT

77   96   40

80   96   39

78   93   38

80   94   39

CLASH

79   39

80   40

78   40

78   38

95   39

96   40

94   37

94   38

NEUTRAL

39   25

38   17

40   26

38   18

98   97   39

101   39   100

39   101   97

98   99   39

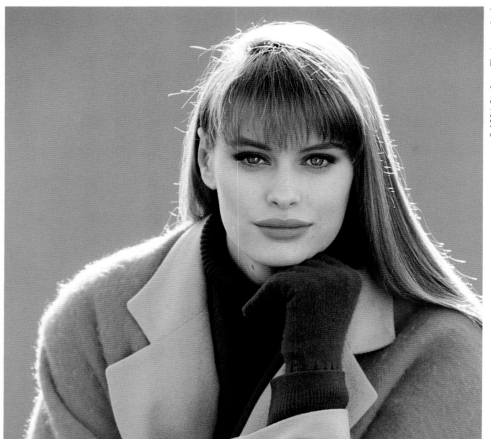

Trendy

What's "in" today may be "out" tomorrow. Trendy color schemes can be pleasantly shocking in combination with other colors. Chartreuse is an excellent example of an accent color used in youthful and offbeat objects. This brilliant hue takes part in countless successful color combinations used in fashion, from basketball shoes to sweaters. A combination of exquisite contrast is yellow-green or chartreuse paired with its perfect complement, magenta.

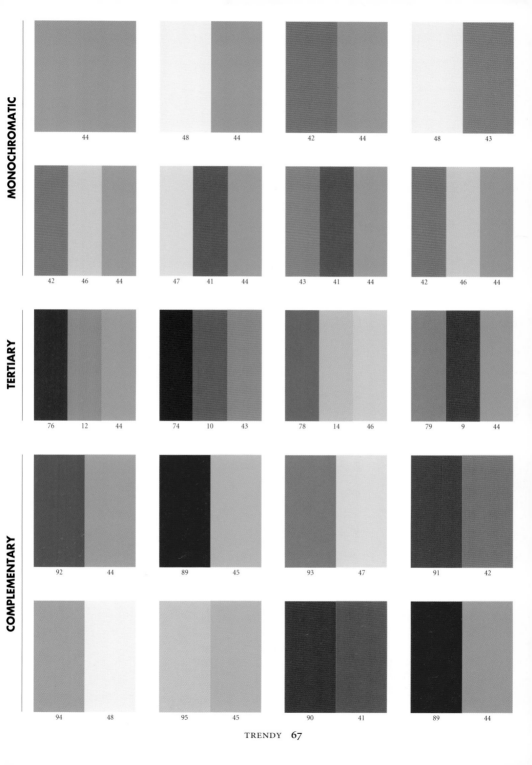

MONOCHROMATIC

44

48 44

42 44

48 43

42 46 44

47 41 44

43 41 44

42 46 44

TERTIARY

76 12 44

74 10 43

78 14 46

79 9 44

COMPLEMENTARY

92 44

89 45

93 47

91 42

94 48

95 45

90 41

89 44

| 28 | 36 | 44 |

| 28 | 39 | 44 |

| 25 | 39 | 44 |

| 25 | 37 | 44 |

| 36 | 44 | 52 |

| 36 | 45 | 52 |

| 39 | 47 | 52 |

| 40 | 43 | 54 |

| 44 | 52 | 60 |

| 41 | 53 | 60 |

| 45 | 55 | 60 |

| 47 | 50 | 60 |

| 84 | 44 | 4 |

| 82 | 44 | 6 |

| 86 | 44 | 7 |

| 87 | 42 | 4 |

| 43 | 84 | 4 |

| 45 | 86 | 2 |

| 42 | 84 | 1 |

| 48 | 84 | 6 |

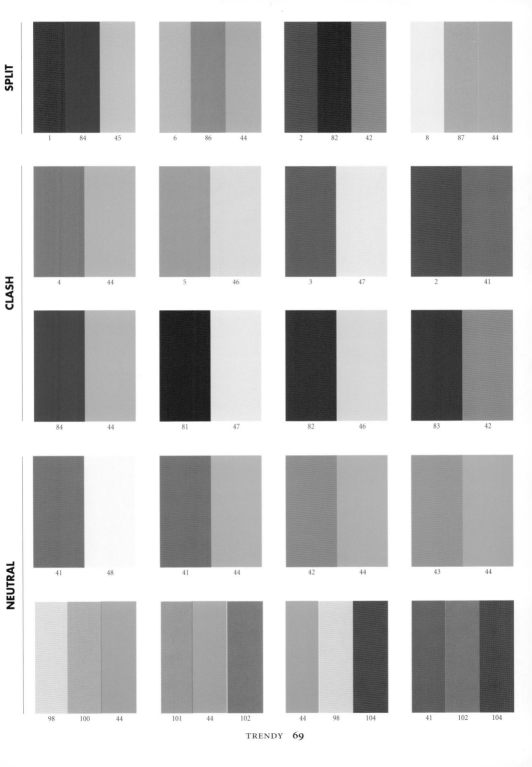

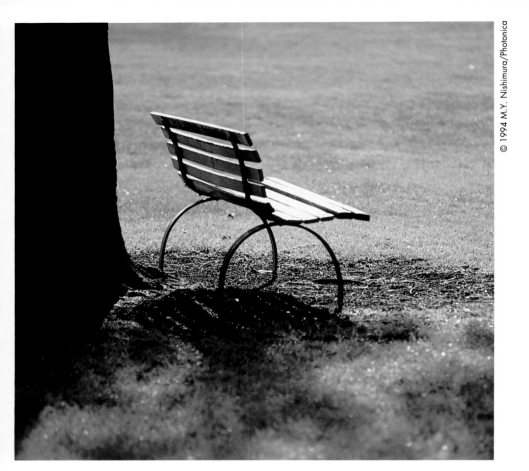

Fresh

Possessing equal amounts of blue and yellow, green suggests health and prosperity. Although weak in its softest tints, green, a recessive hue, only needs to be combined with small amounts of its strong complement, red, to increase its vitality. Using colors analogous to green on the color wheel will create strong color combinations that resemble vivid, outdoor environments. Like newly mowed grass on a clear day, sky blue and green always look fresh and natural together.

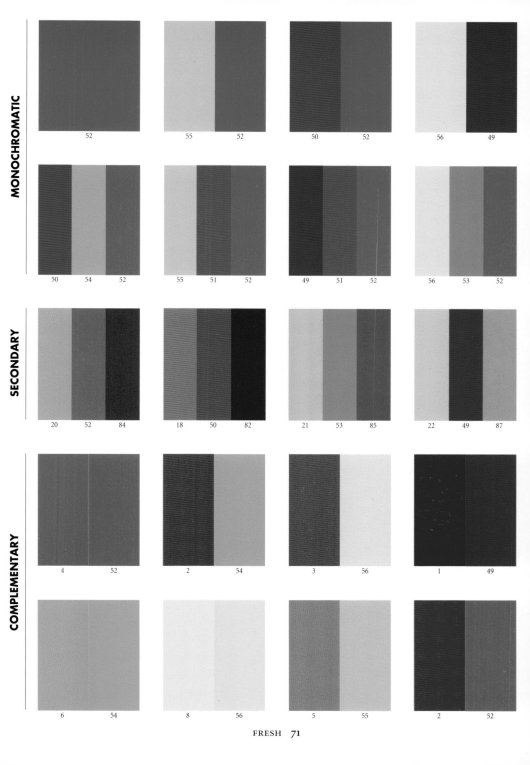

MONOCHROMATIC

52

55   52

50   52

56   49

50   54   52

55   51   52

49   51   52

56   53   52

SECONDARY

20   52   84

18   50   82

21   53   85

22   49   87

COMPLEMENTARY

4   52

2   54

3   56

1   49

6   54

8   56

5   55

2   52

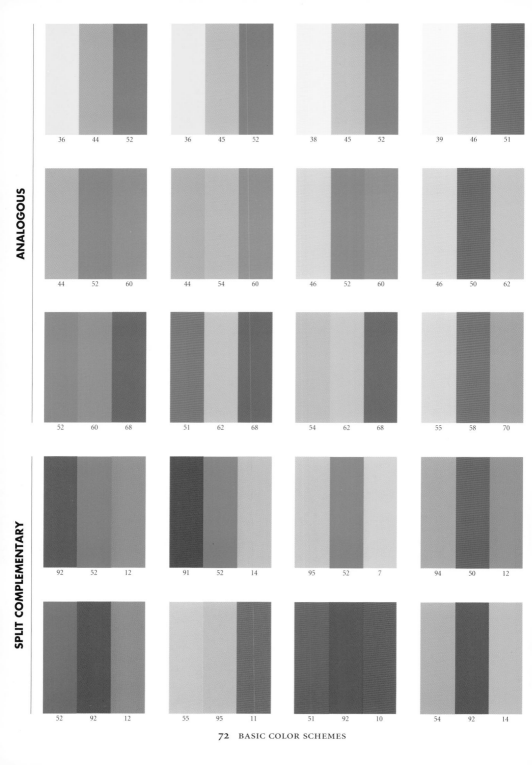

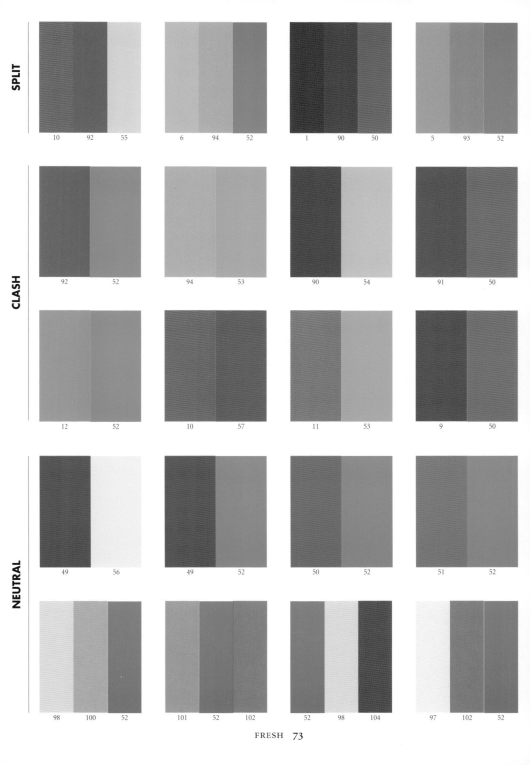

SPLIT

10	92	55
6	94	52
1	90	50
5	93	52

CLASH

92	52
94	53
90	54
91	50

12	52
10	57
11	53
9	50

NEUTRAL

49	56
49	52
50	52
51	52

98	100	52
101	52	102
52	98	104
97	102	52

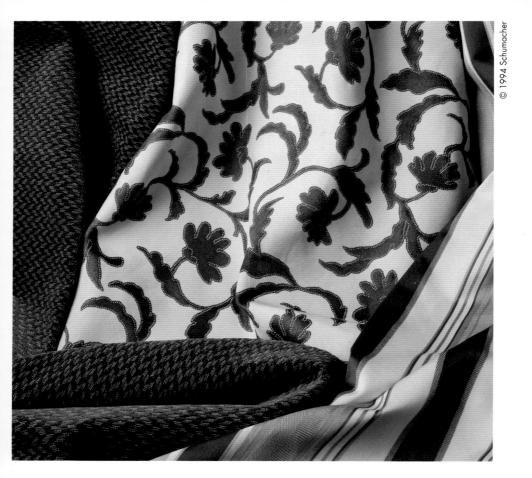

Traditional

Traditional color combinations are often copied from those with historical significance. Conservative colors of blue, burgundy, tan, and green in their grayed or deepened hues, express traditional themes. For example: green, in both its full hue and grayed shades, always signi-fies possession. Hunter green combined with deep gold or burgundy, or in combination with black, suggests richness and stability. Hunter green is frequently seen in the decor of banks and legal offices, where it suggests permanence and value.

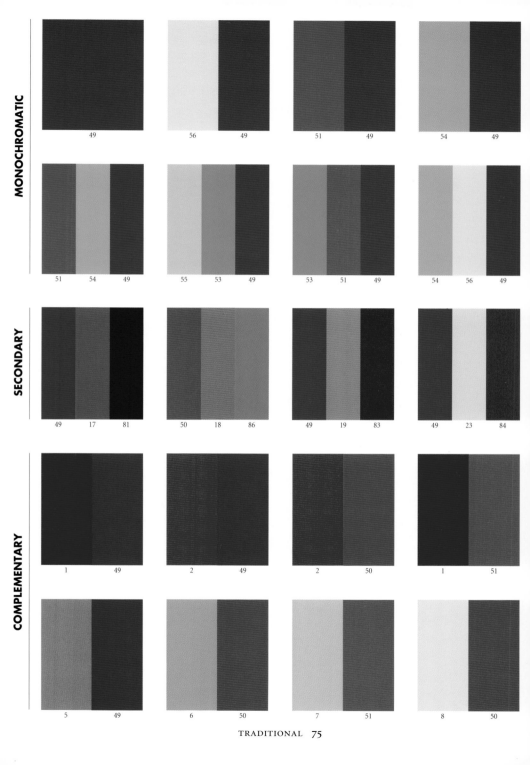

MONOCHROMATIC

49

56   49

51   49

54   49

51   54   49

55   53   49

53   51   49

54   56   49

SECONDARY

49   17   81

50   18   86

49   19   83

49   23   84

COMPLEMENTARY

1   49

2   49

2   50

1   51

5   49

6   50

7   51

8   50

TRADITIONAL   75

33	41	49

34	42	49

38	43	50

34	47	48

41	49	57

42	50	58

47	49	58

48	50	63

49	57	65

50	58	66

49	59	66

49	61	71

9	49	89

10	50	90

13	49	91

14	51	90

14	50	95

16	49	90

15	50	89

13	51	89

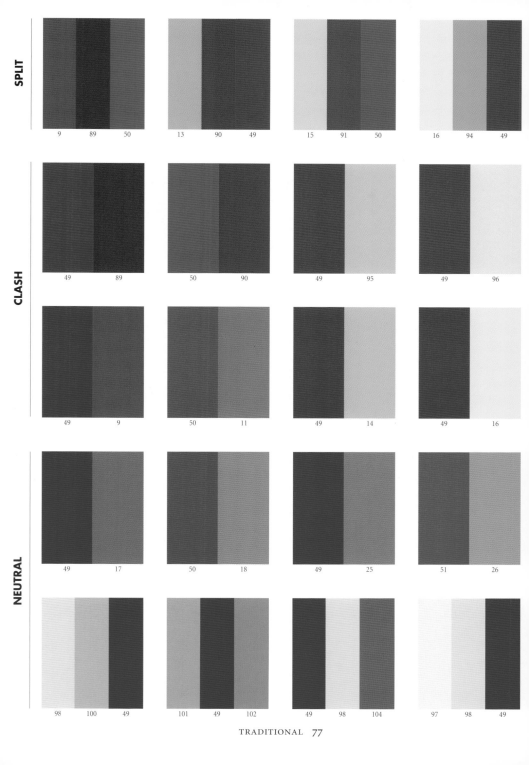

SPLIT

9 89 50   13 90 49   15 91 50   16 94 49

CLASH

49 89   50 90   49 95   49 96

49 9   50 11   49 14   49 16

NEUTRAL

49 17   50 18   49 25   51 26

98 100 49   101 49 102   49 98 104   97 98 49

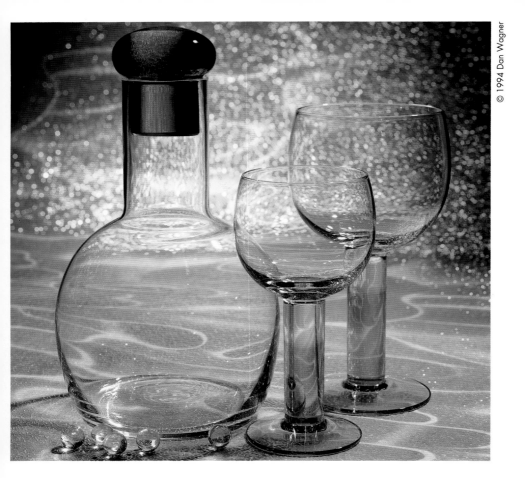

Refreshing

Color combinations that are considered refreshing usually include cool blue-green paired with its complement, red-orange. Blue-green, or teal, is fresh and invigorating. It is frequently used in its full hue to depict travel and leisure. Refreshing color combinations sparkle with lightness while providing a sense of soothing calm.

MONOCHROMATIC

60

62 60

58 60

64 59

59 61 60

62 57 60

58 57 60

59 63 60

TERTIARY

60 28 92

59 27 91

61 29 93

62 27 92

COMPLEMENTARY

12 60

11 62

12 61

9 57

14 61

16 64

10 58

11 62

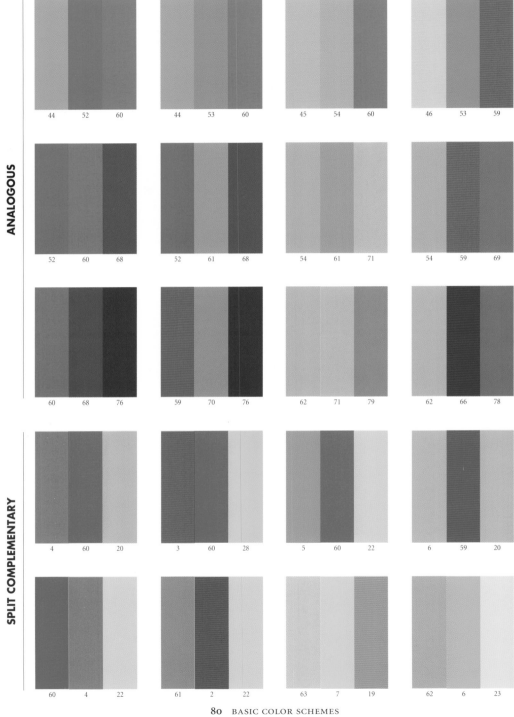

ANALOGOUS

44	52	60
44	53	60
45	54	60
46	53	59

52	60	68
52	61	68
54	61	71
54	59	69

60	68	76
59	70	76
62	71	79
62	66	78

SPLIT COMPLEMENTARY

4	60	20
3	60	28
5	60	22
6	59	20

60	4	22
61	2	22
63	7	19
62	6	23

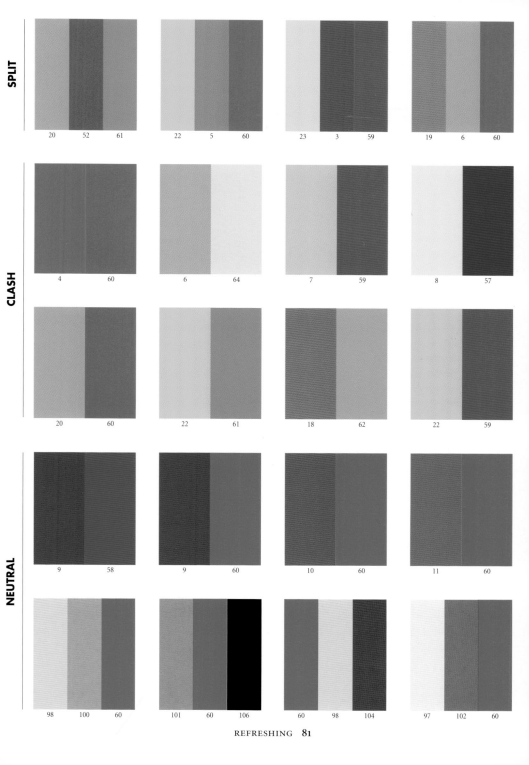

SPLIT

20 52 61
22 5 60
23 3 59
19 6 60

CLASH

4 60
6 64
7 59
8 57

20 60
22 61
18 62
22 59

NEUTRAL

9 58
9 60
10 60
11 60

98 100 60
101 60 106
60 98 104
97 102 60

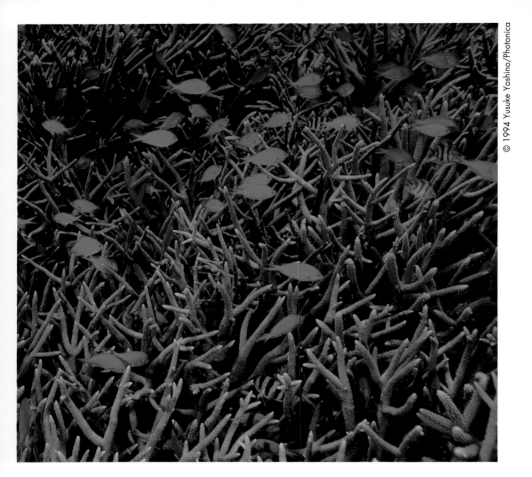

© 1994 Yusuke Yoshino/Photonica

Tropical

Tropical hues on the color wheel always include turquoise. Blue-green is lightened to turquoise by the addition of white and is the warmest of the cool colors. Staying with the lightest tints of the blue-green family will increase the feeling and message of tranquility.

Using red-orange, the complement of turquoise, is perfect in any of these combinations. Like flowers in nature, these color schemes enhance any setting and create a serene and stress-free feeling.

82   BASIC COLOR SCHEMES

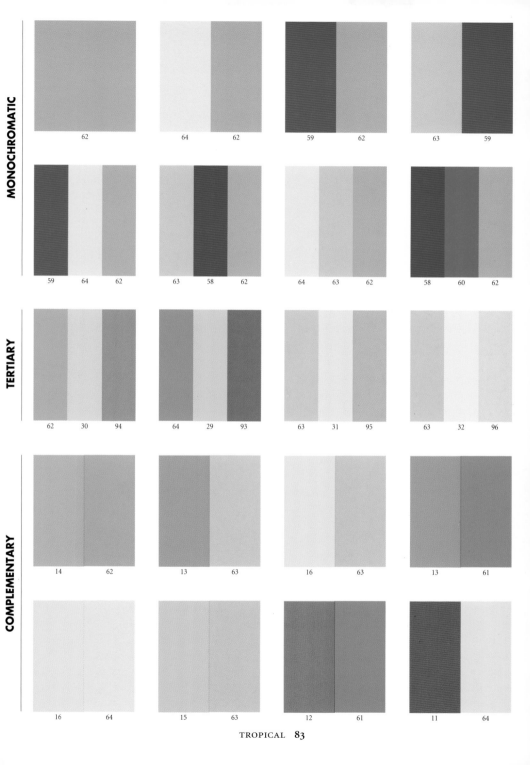

MONOCHROMATIC

62

64 62

59 62

63 59

59 64 62

63 58 62

64 63 62

58 60 62

TERTIARY

62 30 94

64 29 93

63 31 95

63 32 96

COMPLEMENTARY

14 62

13 63

16 63

13 61

16 64

15 63

12 61

11 64

ANALOGOUS

46	54	62
45	55	62
48	55	64
47	53	62

54	62	70
53	63	69
56	63	72
55	61	71

62	70	78
61	71	79
64	72	80
63	69	79

SPLIT COMPLEMENTARY

6	62	22
5	62	23
7	62	24
8	63	22

21	62	6
20	63	7
22	64	6
24	64	8

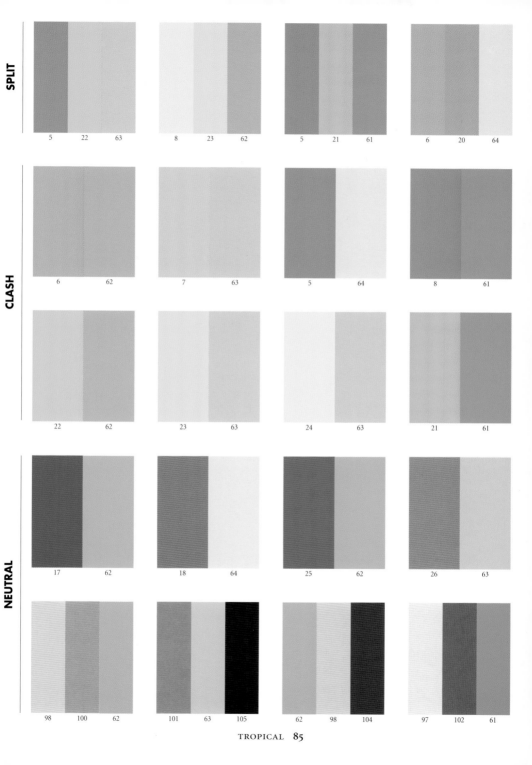

SPLIT

5 22 63
8 23 62
5 21 61
6 20 64

CLASH

6 62
7 63
5 64
8 61

22 62
23 63
24 63
21 61

NEUTRAL

17 62
18 64
25 62
26 63

98 100 62
101 63 105
62 98 104
97 102 61

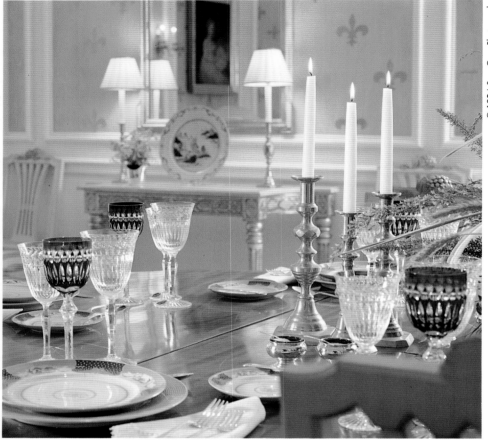

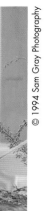

Classic

Classic color combinations are indicative of strength and authority. Intense royal blue is the centerpiece of any classic grouping of colors. It stands out, even when combined with other hues.

Classic combinations imply truth, responsibility, and trust. Because of its proximity to green, royal blue evokes a sense of continuity, stability, and strength, especially in combination with its split complement red-orange and yellow-orange.

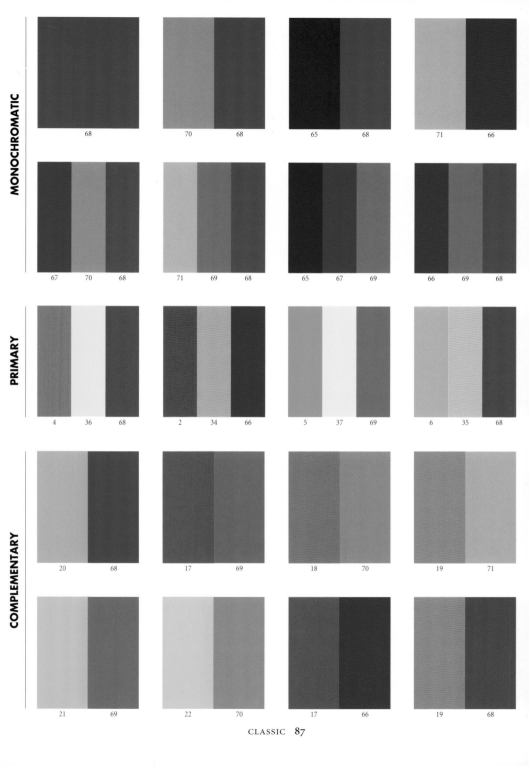

MONOCHROMATIC

68

70 68

65 68

71 66

67 70 68

71 69 68

65 67 69

66 69 68

PRIMARY

4 36 68

2 34 66

5 37 69

6 35 68

COMPLEMENTARY

20 68

17 69

18 70

19 71

21 69

22 70

17 66

19 68

52 60 68   52 61 68   54 62 68   53 62 66

60 68 76   60 69 76   62 70 76   61 67 78

68 76 84   67 77 84   71 78 84   72 75 87

12 68 28   10 68 29   14 68 29   15 67 28

66 28 12   69 29 11   67 28 10   70 28 14

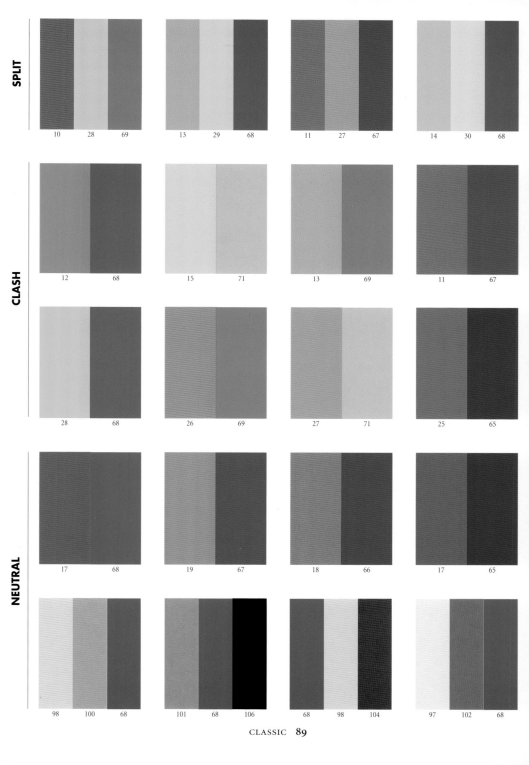

SPLIT

10	28	69
13	29	68
11	27	67
14	30	68

CLASH

12	68
15	71
13	69
11	67

28	68
26	69
27	71
25	65

NEUTRAL

17	68
19	67
18	66
17	65

98	100	68
101	68	106
68	98	104
97	102	68

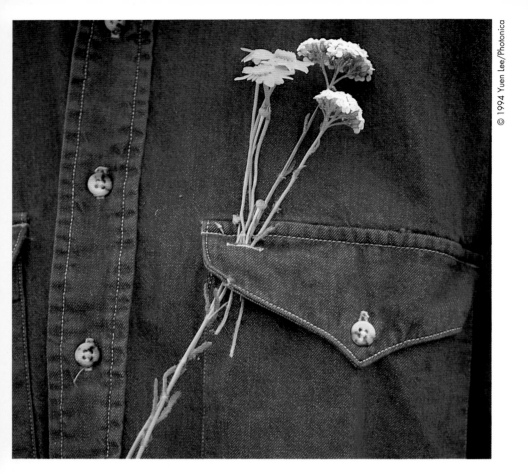

Dependable

One of the most widely accepted hues is navy blue. Combinations using this color are interpreted as dependable and reliable. They also carry an undeniable message of authority. Police officers, naval officers, and court officers wear color combinations that include deep, secure navy blue in order to command authority through their appearance. When accented with red and gold, navy becomes less stern, but still communicates firmness and strength.

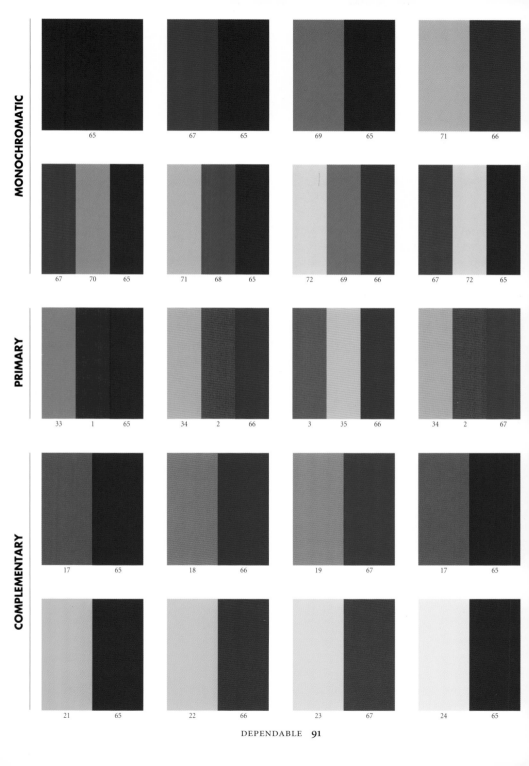

MONOCHROMATIC

65

67   65

69   65

71   66

67   70   65

71   68   65

72   69   66

67   72   65

PRIMARY

33   1   65

34   2   66

3   35   66

34   2   67

COMPLEMENTARY

17   65

18   66

19   67

17   65

21   65

22   66

23   67

24   65

DEPENDABLE   91

49   57   65   50   59   65   51   61   66   50   62   67

57   66   78   58   69   76   61   67   74   63   65   78

66   75   82   65   77   83   66   76   86   65   79   84

10   65   26   9   66   27   11   65   26   10   66   25

14   65   26   14   65   32   15   66   31   9   65   32

92 BASIC COLOR SCHEMES

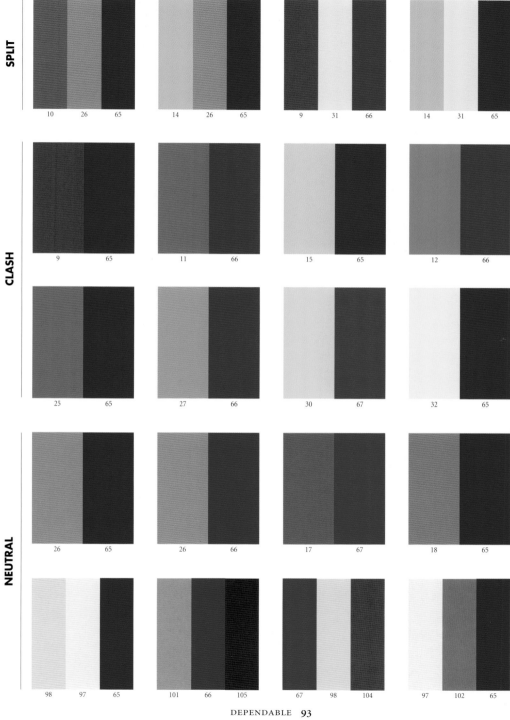

SPLIT

| 10 | 26 | 65 | | 14 | 26 | 65 | | 9 | 31 | 66 | | 14 | 31 | 65 |

CLASH

| 9 | 65 | | 11 | 66 | | 15 | 65 | | 12 | 66 |

| 25 | 65 | | 27 | 66 | | 30 | 67 | | 32 | 65 |

NEUTRAL

| 26 | 65 | | 26 | 66 | | 17 | 67 | | 18 | 65 |

| 98 | 97 | 65 | | 101 | 66 | 105 | | 67 | 98 | 104 | | 97 | 102 | 65 |

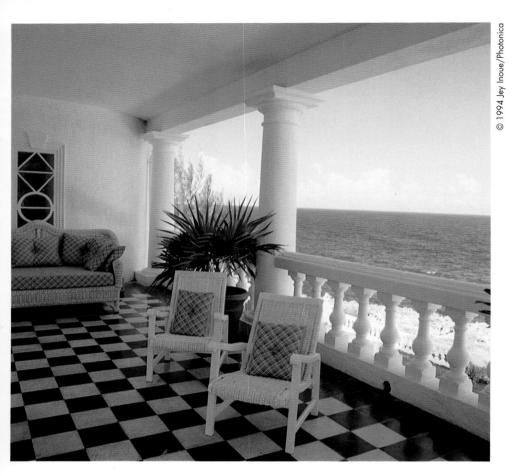

Calm

In any stressful environment, combining grayed or lightened tints of blue will produce a calming and restful effect. Lightened blue is at the center of color schemes that reassure and are considered truthful and direct.

Cool colors with tints can maintain a sense of well-being and peace. It is important that the complements and accents of these tranquil hues are similar in value, as hues which are too vivid can create unwanted tension.

MONOCHROMATIC

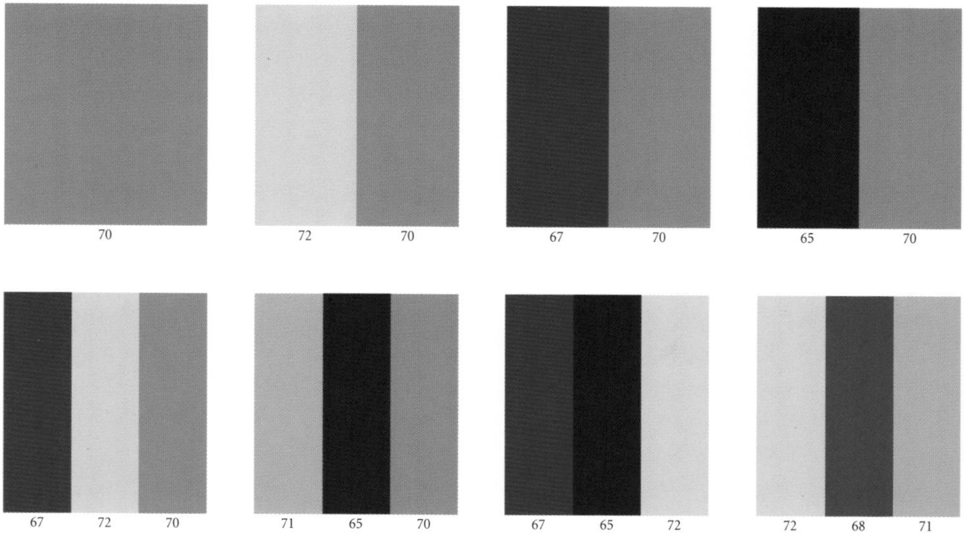

PRIMARY

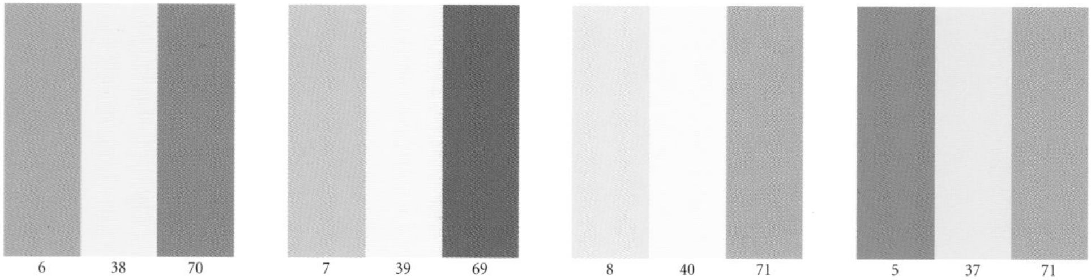

COMPLEMENTARY

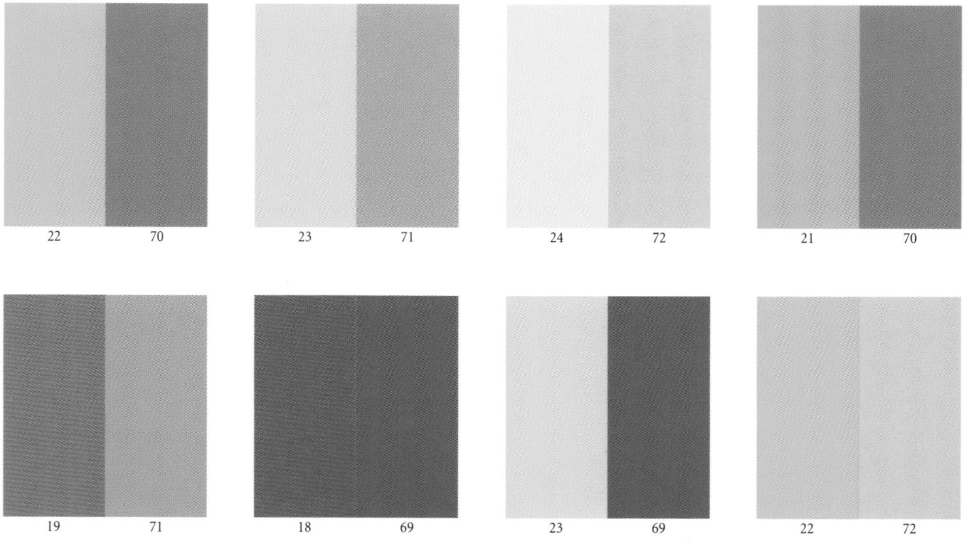

| 54 | 62 | 70 | | 53 | 63 | 71 | | 56 | 63 | 70 | | 55 | 61 | 72 |

| 62 | 70 | 78 | | 64 | 71 | 78 | | 61 | 70 | 79 | | 64 | 72 | 80 |

| 70 | 78 | 86 | | 69 | 79 | 88 | | 71 | 78 | 88 | | 70 | 80 | 87 |

| 30 | 70 | 14 | | 31 | 71 | 15 | | 32 | 72 | 16 | | 29 | 70 | 13 |

| 31 | 71 | 14 | | 29 | 71 | 15 | | 32 | 72 | 14 | | 30 | 70 | 14 |

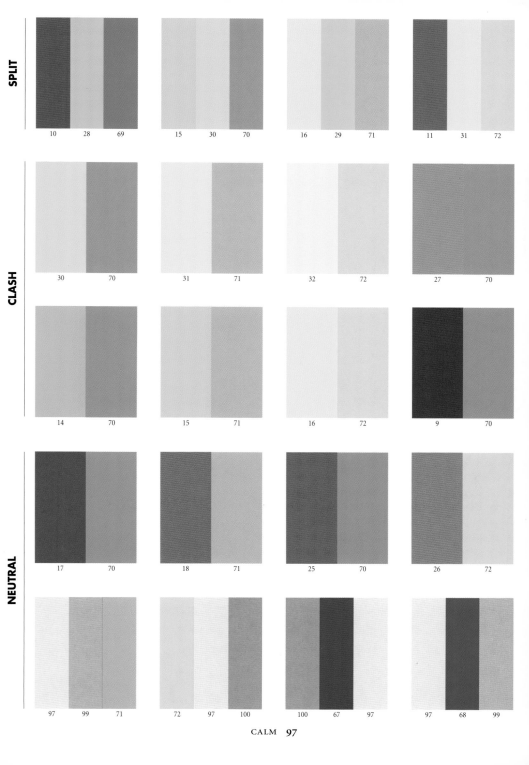

SPLIT

10 28 69   15 30 70   16 29 71   11 31 72

CLASH

30 70   31 71   32 72   27 70

14 70   15 71   16 72   9 70

NEUTRAL

17 70   18 71   25 70   26 72

97 99 71   72 97 100   100 67 97   97 68 99

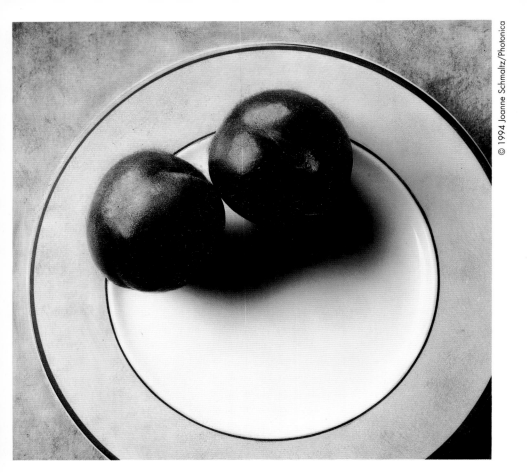

Regal

The fullness of blue combined with the power of red creates blue-violet. It is the darkest hue on the color wheel and contains no black to diminish its innate power.

Combinations using this color symbolize authority and regal inspiration. Likened to the deepest blue-black plums of summer, blue-violet combined with its complement, yellow-orange, creates a most striking color scheme. This lush combination suggests royalty and is seldom used outside a daunting environment.

MONOCHROMATIC

| 76 | | 78 | 76 | | 73 | 76 | | 79 | 75 |

| 74 | 77 | 76 | | 79 | 75 | 76 | | 77 | 73 | 79 | | 73 | 80 | 76 |

TERTIARY

| 12 | 44 | 76 | | 11 | 43 | 75 | | 12 | 45 | 78 | | 14 | 75 | 76 |

COMPLEMENTARY

| 28 | 76 | | 27 | 78 | | 26 | 80 | | 25 | 75 |

| 30 | 78 | | 31 | 79 | | 27 | 74 | | 26 | 76 |

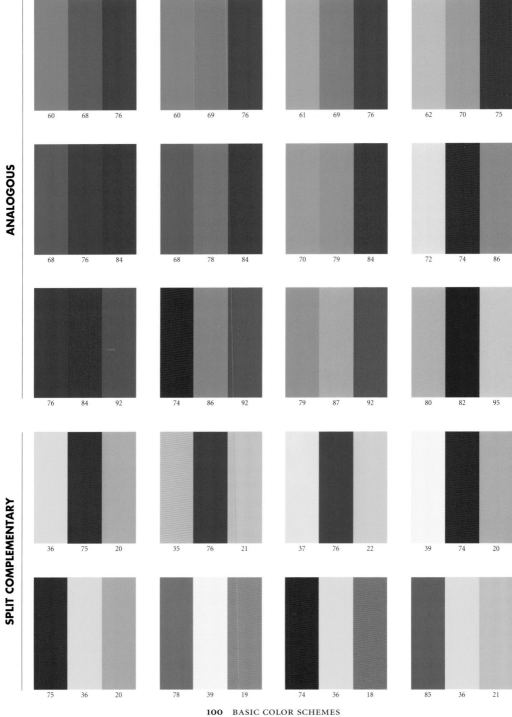

ANALOGOUS

60	68	76
60	69	76
61	69	76
62	70	75

68	76	84
68	78	84
70	79	84
72	74	86

76	84	92
74	86	92
79	87	92
80	82	95

SPLIT COMPLEMENTARY

36	75	20
35	76	21
37	76	22
39	74	20

75	36	20
78	39	19
74	36	18
85	36	21

100 BASIC COLOR SCHEMES

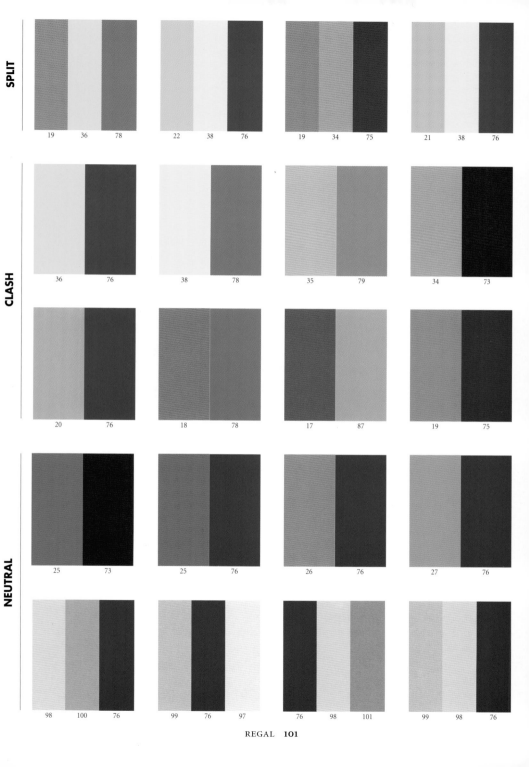

SPLIT

19 36 78

22 38 76

19 34 75

21 38 76

CLASH

36 76

38 78

35 79

34 73

20 76

18 78

17 87

19 75

NEUTRAL

25 73

25 76

26 76

27 76

98 100 76

99 76 97

76 98 101

99 98 76

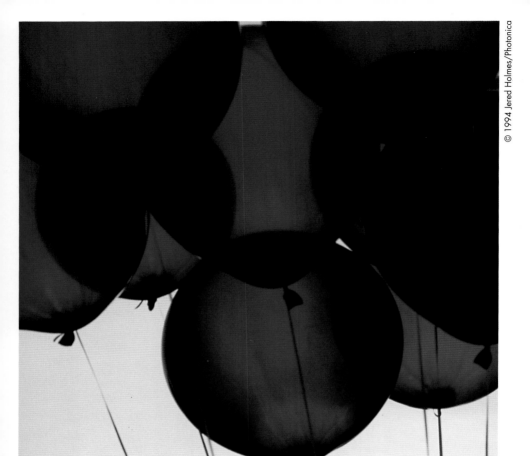

Magical

Elements of surprise and magic are often associated with violet. By itself, violet conveys its own unpredictable personality. With its secondary partners, orange and green, violet in any tint or shade becomes part of an exciting team, which is slightly offbeat.

When used with chartreuse and yellow-orange, it is whimsical and clashing, even loud. In combination with its true complement yellow, violet has spectral balance and can be enjoyed for extended periods of time. In fashion, it is considered an immature color and is used to bridge the gap between child and adult.

84

86　84

81　84

87　83

81　87　84

86　82　84

87　86　84

82　88　84

52　84　20

49　83　18

53　87　22

55　82　20

36　84

35　87

34　86

33　88

40　87

38　86

35　83

34　84

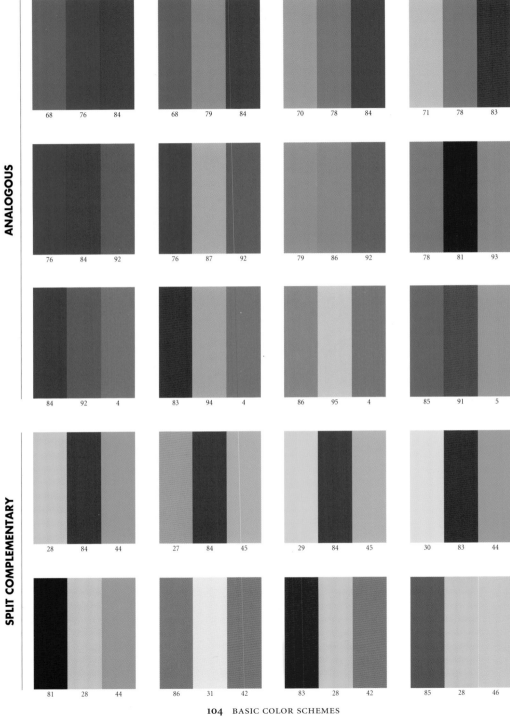

| 68 | 76 | 84 |

| 68 | 79 | 84 |

| 70 | 78 | 84 |

| 71 | 78 | 83 |

| 76 | 84 | 92 |

| 76 | 87 | 92 |

| 79 | 86 | 92 |

| 78 | 81 | 93 |

| 84 | 92 | 4 |

| 83 | 94 | 4 |

| 86 | 95 | 4 |

| 85 | 91 | 5 |

| 28 | 84 | 44 |

| 27 | 84 | 45 |

| 29 | 84 | 45 |

| 30 | 83 | 44 |

| 81 | 28 | 44 |

| 86 | 31 | 42 |

| 83 | 28 | 42 |

| 85 | 28 | 46 |

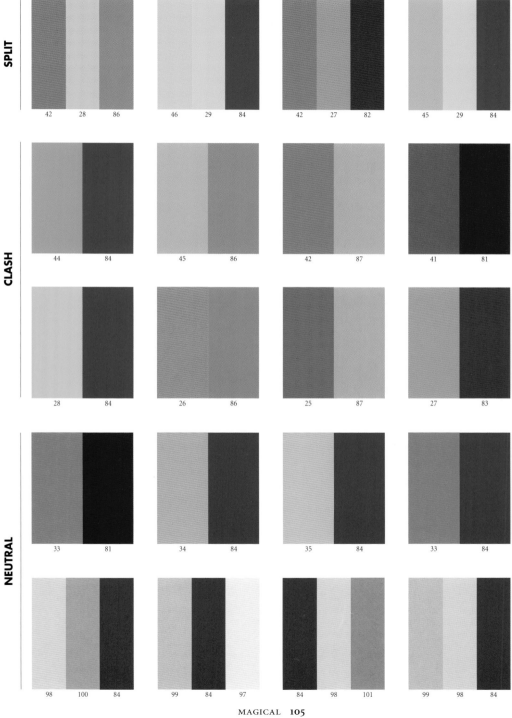

SPLIT

CLASH

NEUTRAL

42	28	86
46	29	84
42	27	82
45	29	84

44	84
45	86
42	87
41	81

28	84
26	86
25	87
27	83

33	81
34	84
35	84
33	84

98	100	84
99	84	97
84	98	101
99	98	84

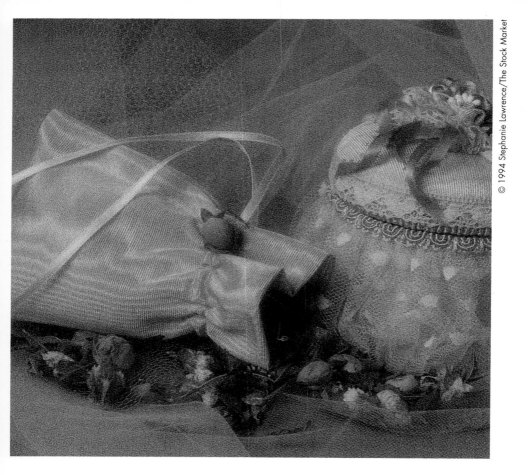

Nostalgic

Color combinations using lavender are often thought of as nostalgic. They are reminiscent of the Victorian era and can remind us of dreamy moments, poetry, and romantic ideals. More delicate and less passionate than pink, lavender has red and blue in its violet makeup. When combined with other pastels, lavender is the prominent hue, even with its muted accents.

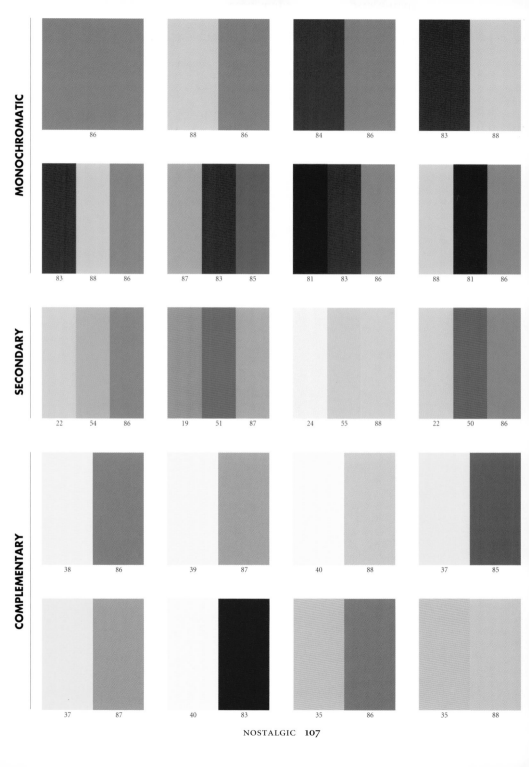

MONOCHROMATIC

86

88 86

84 86

83 88

83 88 86

87 83 85

81 83 86

88 81 86

SECONDARY

22 54 86

19 51 87

24 55 88

22 50 86

COMPLEMENTARY

38 86

39 87

40 88

37 85

37 87

40 83

35 86

35 88

ANALOGOUS

| 70 | 78 | 86 | | 69 | 79 | 86 | | 72 | 79 | 88 | | 71 | 77 | 83 |

| 78 | 86 | 94 | | 77 | 86 | 95 | | 80 | 85 | 92 | | 79 | 88 | 94 |

| 86 | 94 | 6 | | 85 | 95 | 8 | | 87 | 93 | 5 | | 88 | 95 | 7 |

SPLIT COMPLEMENTARY

| 46 | 86 | 30 | | 48 | 87 | 31 | | 42 | 86 | 31 | | 47 | 86 | 27 |

| 41 | 83 | 27 | | 42 | 85 | 32 | | 46 | 87 | 31 | | 43 | 85 | 26 |

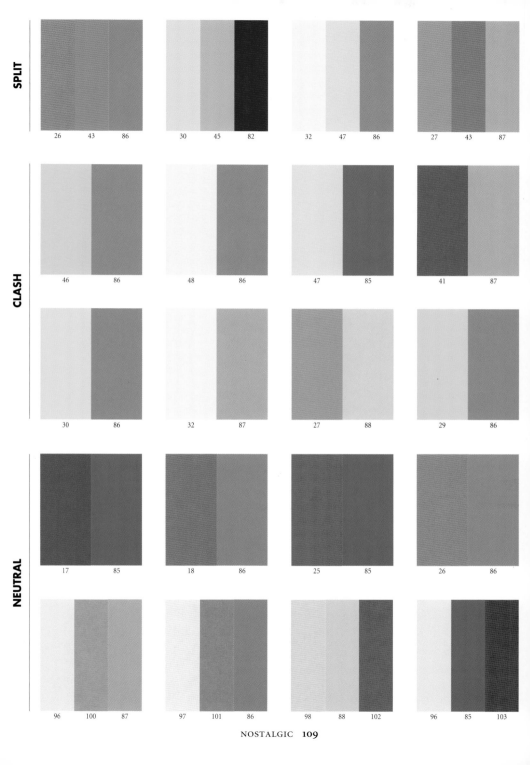

SPLIT

26 43 86

30 45 82

32 47 86

27 43 87

CLASH

46 86

48 86

47 85

41 87

30 86

32 87

27 88

29 86

NEUTRAL

17 85

18 86

25 85

26 86

96 100 87

97 101 86

98 88 102

96 85 103

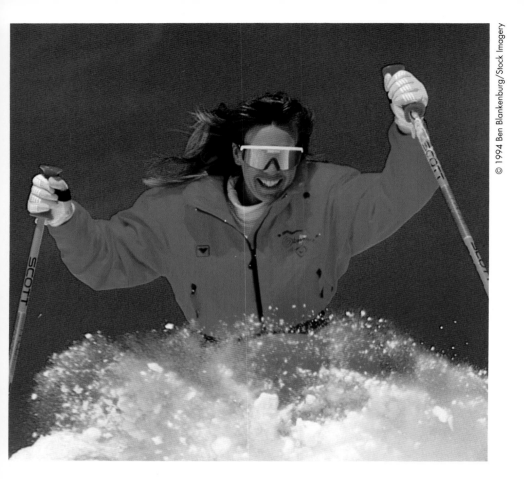

Energetic

Color combinations that are energetic often contain red-violet, also known as fuchsia. It always sends an unmistakable message of activity. Fuchsia, or magenta, has such an exuberant personality that in order to be workable it is often combined with its complementary hue, chartreuse. A clash combination using fuchsia and yellow or green will be exciting for the moment, but will invariably limit the overall effect of the combination and lessen its workability. Yellow-green, when paired with fuchsia or magenta, heightens the enthusiastic personality of this energetic color.

MONOCHROMATIC

92

94   92

91   92

95   90

90   96   92

96   90   92

89   91   93

91   95   92

TERTIARY

28   92   60

26   94   59

29   94   61

31   91   60

COMPLEMENTARY

44   92

42   94

43   93

42   91

45   95

47   96

41   90

42   92

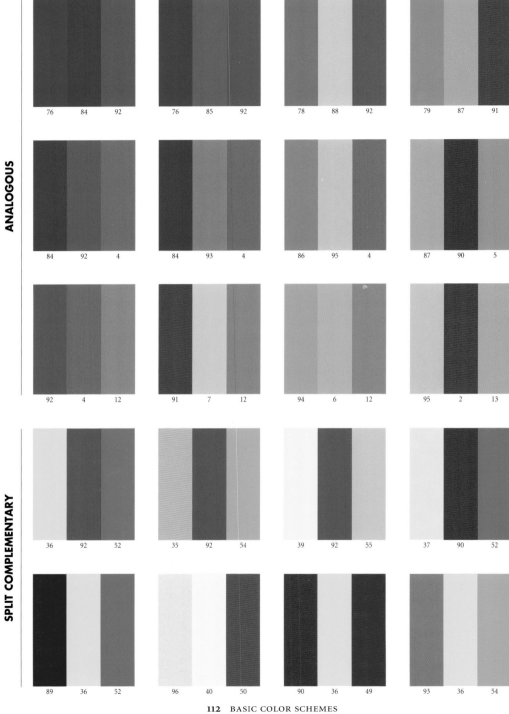

76	84	92
76	85	92
78	88	92
79	87	91

84	92	4
84	93	4
86	95	4
87	90	5

92	4	12
91	7	12
94	6	12
95	2	13

36	92	52
35	92	54
39	92	55
37	90	52

89	36	52
96	40	50
90	36	49
93	36	54

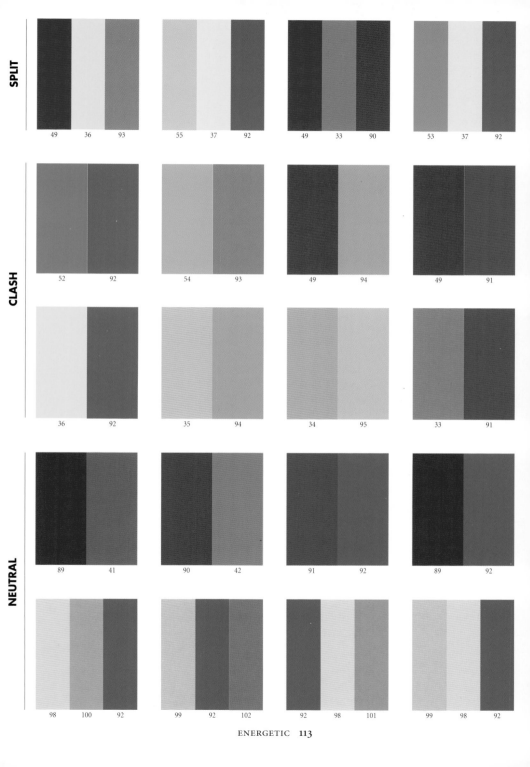

SPLIT

49   36   93

55   37   92

49   33   90

53   37   92

CLASH

52   92

54   93

49   94

49   91

36   92

35   94

34   95

33   91

NEUTRAL

89   41

90   42

91   92

89   92

98   100   92

99   92   102

92   98   101

99   98   92

Subdued

Unlike an energetic color scheme, a subdued or grayed scheme has little contrast. Mauve, a blend of magenta, gray, and white, is a diminished color. The addition of minimal gray and white to any brilliant hue results in subdued and delicate variations, including grayed blues and grayed greens. Mauve combined with other tints and shades appears to be understated and dull. A spark of color in the form of its complement, or a more vivid tone of the original hue, must be added to bring these mellow hues back to life. To maintain the subdued nature of similar colors, shades should be used sparingly.

94

94   96

92   94

91   94

96   92   94

89   92   95

90   96   94

96   95   94

62   30   94

63   32   95

26   59   94

29   60   93

46   94

48   94

42   95

45   95

48   96

43   90

42   94

47   91

78	86	94	77	87	94	80	85	95	75	86	94

| 86 | 94 | 6 | 85 | 95 | 8 | 88 | 95 | 5 | 86 | 92 | 7 |

| 94 | 6 | 13 | 93 | 7 | 15 | 96 | 6 | 14 | 95 | 7 | 16 |

| 55 | 95 | 39 | 54 | 95 | 40 | 56 | 94 | 38 | 54 | 93 | 38 |

| 51 | 91 | 38 | 54 | 93 | 34 | 55 | 95 | 35 | 50 | 96 | 34 |

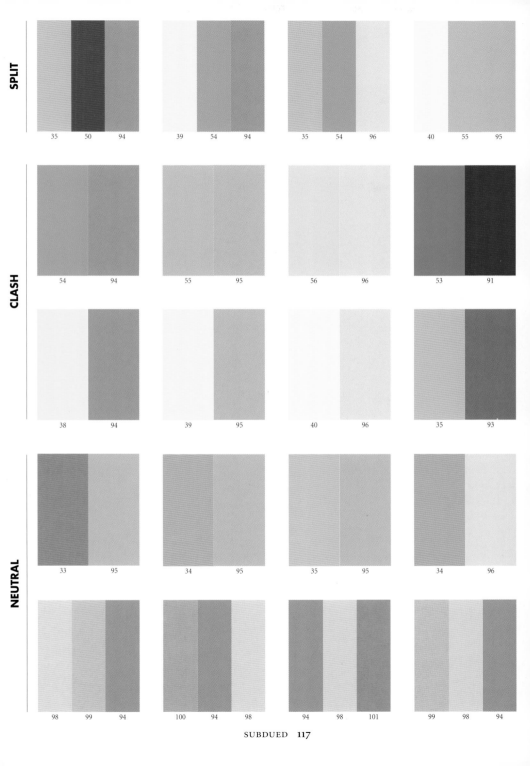

SPLIT

| 35 | 50 | 94 | | 39 | 54 | 94 | | 35 | 54 | 96 | | 40 | 55 | 95 |

CLASH

| 54 | 94 | | 55 | 95 | | 56 | 96 | | 53 | 91 |

| 38 | 94 | | 39 | 95 | | 40 | 96 | | 35 | 93 |

NEUTRAL

| 33 | 95 | | 34 | 95 | | 35 | 95 | | 34 | 96 |

| 98 | 99 | 94 | | 100 | 94 | 98 | | 94 | 98 | 101 | | 99 | 98 | 94 |

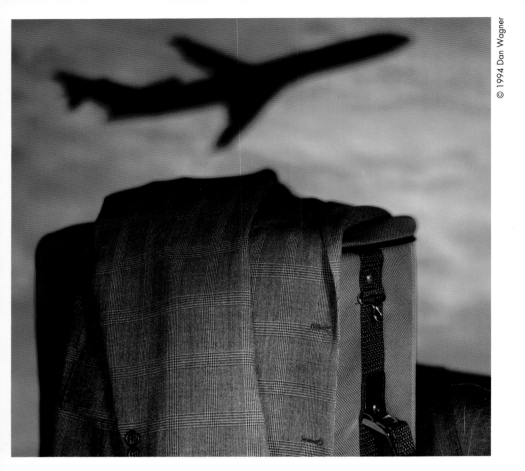

Professional

In the world of the business professional, color is evaluated with scrutiny. In fashion, the word "professional" has come to mean grays and tonal blacks because these colors lack personal characteristics and are truly neutral. Warmed grays, however, are perfect backgrounds for brilliant hues such as red, teal, or orange. Schemes based on achromatic gray combined with vivid accents become accented neutrals.

Gray is unexciting but practical. It sends a sober message, with a minimum of humor.

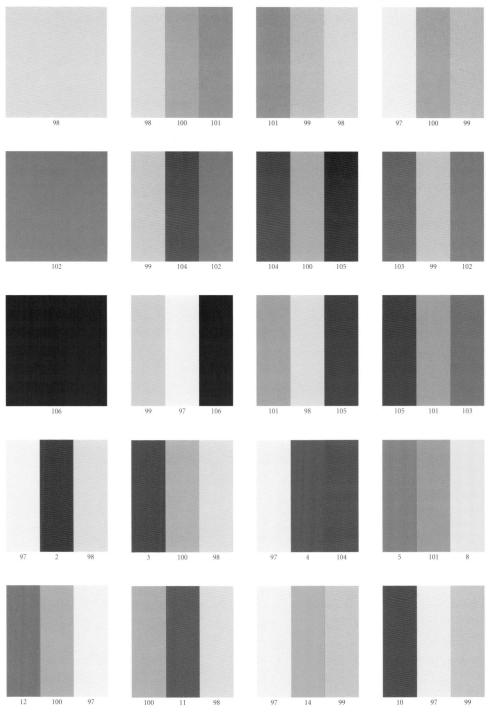

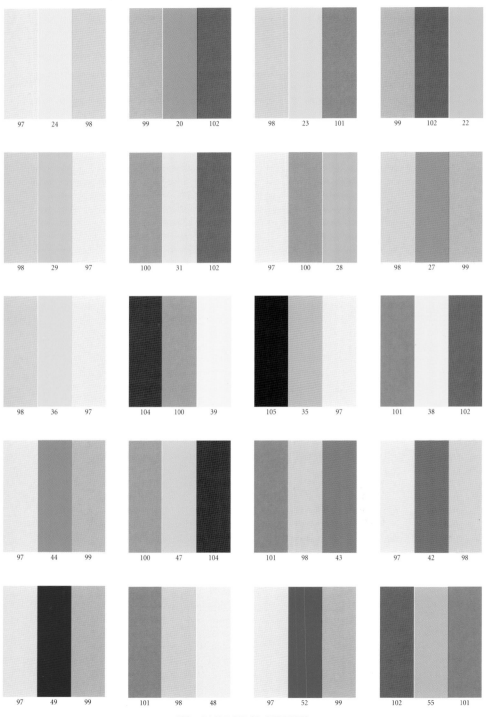

| 97 | 24 | 98 | | 99 | 20 | 102 | | 98 | 23 | 101 | | 99 | 102 | 22 |

| 98 | 29 | 97 | | 100 | 31 | 102 | | 97 | 100 | 28 | | 98 | 27 | 99 |

| 98 | 36 | 97 | | 104 | 100 | 39 | | 105 | 35 | 97 | | 101 | 38 | 102 |

| 97 | 44 | 99 | | 100 | 47 | 104 | | 101 | 98 | 43 | | 97 | 42 | 98 |

| 97 | 49 | 99 | | 101 | 98 | 48 | | 97 | 52 | 99 | | 102 | 55 | 101 |

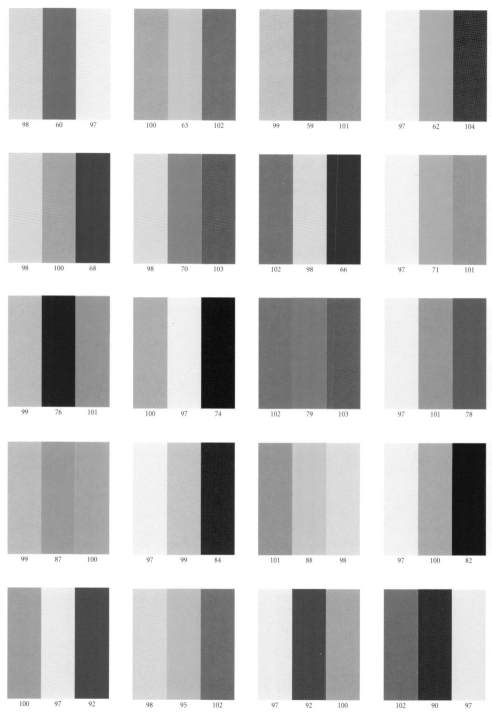

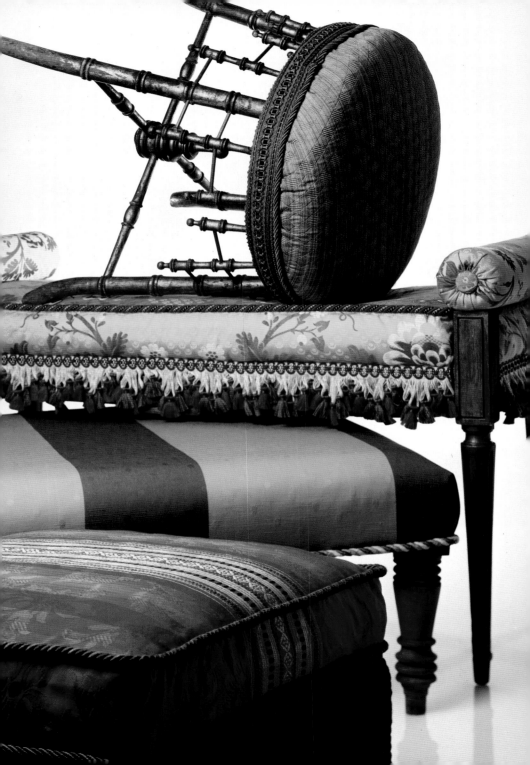

Color Trends

WHAT ARE COLOR TRENDS?

Professionals in the fields of color research, color merchandising, advertising and marketing, as well as the related professions of graphic design, fashion, interior design, and industrial design, make selections and reach a consensus on which colors will be successful and fashionable for the coming years. This color forecasting translates into "color trends." For example, the orange shag rugs of the sixties and the avocado refrigerators of the seventies were some of the products that reflected the "color trends" of those decades. Along with the current economic and cultural directions of trade markets, product negotiation, median incomes, and social status, decisions about color trends are also based on psychological insight into the use of color. Color choices are vitally important to all retail sales, products, and services. In every industrialized nation, color is big business.

Choosing colors that result in changes for consumer markets is a highly specialized field. An organization involved in setting color trends that impact on a number of industries is the Association for International Color Directions (AICD), located in Alexandria, Virginia. The AICD holds international conferences and workshops to ensure accuracy in tracking predictable color trends. The marketing arm of the AICD, the Color Marketing Group, forecasts ahead three years, allowing ample time to implement the design and manufacture of key industry products in new and definitive colors.

A second organization, the Color Association of the United States (CAUS), located in New York City, specializes in color predictions for fashion, interior design, and environmental industries. A panel of eight to twelve color specialists meets annually to determine the ongoing impact of the current trends. Color trends are closely linked to the economy, and, as a result, advertising and marketing strategies are affected whenever a new color or color combination emerges on the world market. The color trend becomes part of the media vocabulary, sending a "color message" to the world via television and print.

As consumers become comfortable with color in daily life, analysts look for newer and more exciting color combinations to stimulate their emotions and product needs. This is often interpreted as "something new" or "in style." A color scheme that is compatible with one industry may not be pleasing or workable in another. To offset this situation and maintain the accuracy of choice, color analysts will make parallel or specific recommendations for fashion, industry, or interior environmental use.

COLOR TRENDS THEN . . . AND NOW

In general, pastel tints of green, blue, and orange, prominent for decades in most interior products, have recently given way to brilliant colors and warm, subtle shades. Soft and medium tints have been replaced by hues of vivid reds, yellows, and the jewel-like tones of sapphire and amethyst. These hues are seen most often in upscale products such as evening wear and expensive fabrics for the home. They carry an aura of wealth and cultural diversity. Gone are the dark and sophisticated grays of the recent past, they have been replaced by burnished warm metallics of gold and copper, combined with rich, reddish hues of burgundy, terra-cotta, and rust.

The colors prominent today and for the coming years are not flat pastels but

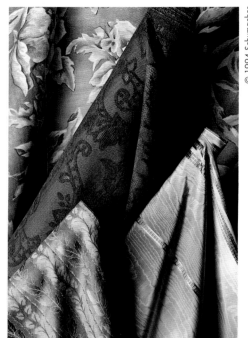

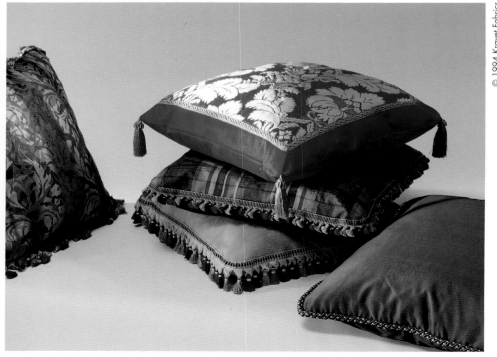

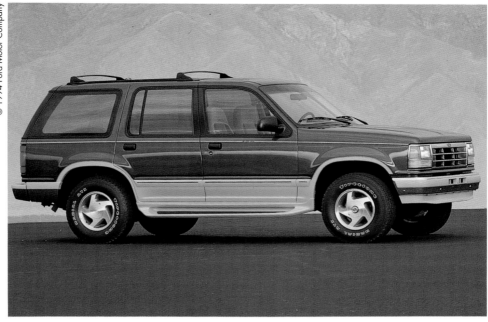

the vibrant tones of magenta, turquoise, and gold. They are used in some manufactured goods, interiors, and fashion. It is accurate to say that reds, greens, and blues in fully saturated color and warm, lustrous, dark shades like burgundy, hunter green, and navy will be strong choices for the fore-seeable future. Red brings excitement to wardrobes, accessories, and luxury items and is a favorite of both men and women. Vibrant deep greens will be used as major color accents in fashion, personal interiors, and places of business. Dark blues and warm terra-cottas will be major color players in restaurants and public places. Accented with a contrasting bright white or creamy yellow-orange, these colors generate a feeling of warm elegance, and enhance interior space.

INDUSTRY

Automobiles continue to reflect deep vibrant hues of blue-green, reds, and warm metallics, a color development indicating an upward economy. When the economy is unstable or on a downward slope, automobiles are usually painted in nondescript but safe colors, such as grays and tans.

Another factor in the equation of color choice in industrial products is the emerging presence of women as "major purchase" buyers. Women now buy automobiles as often as men. Long in demand by the industry, conservative colors are changing to include the more active turquoise and warm metallic. This trend is also reflected in the collateral and complementary color schemes of automobile interiors.

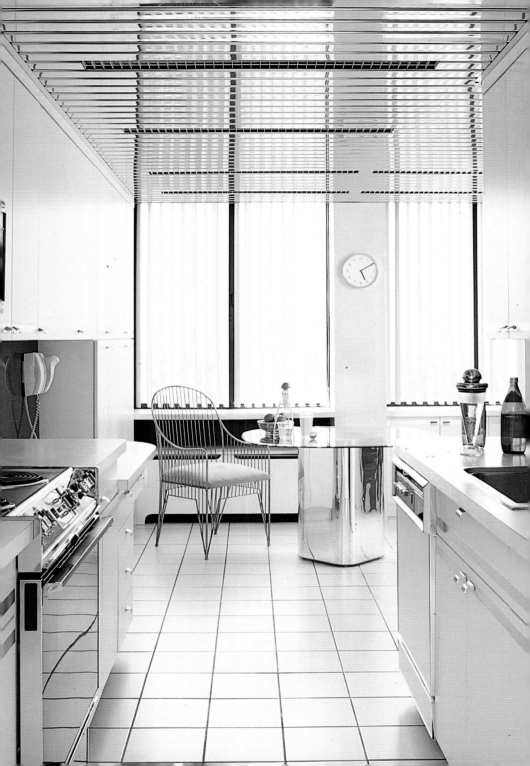

Refrigerators, washers and driers, dishwashers, and major domestic appliances continue to remain sterile white or warm utilitarian pewter. These "noncolors" are becoming increasingly popular as more women spend less time at home. Instead of light pastels, bright glossy white will be used as a dominant hue and as an accent in domestic environments.

FASHION

According to color marketing groups the line between male and female color preference has disappeared. All colors in fashion are now acceptable for men's as well as women's clothing. This trend is evidenced by men confidently wearing brightly colored accessories. Continuing in this direction, fully saturated powerful reds and violets with bluish undertones are the predicted color choices for both sexes.

Forecasters say clothing color, regardless of the season, will be bright with increased sheen, making the matte noncolors of the past obsolete. Although black remains the "color of choice" in apparel for the young adult woman, vivid accessories and outerwear is acceptable. Lots of sparkle and beading in fabrics offsets black's usually hostile personality, giving it a more lively appearance.

Brilliant silks and taffetas in magenta,

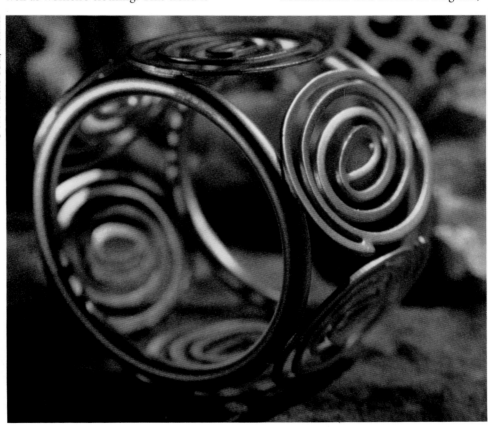

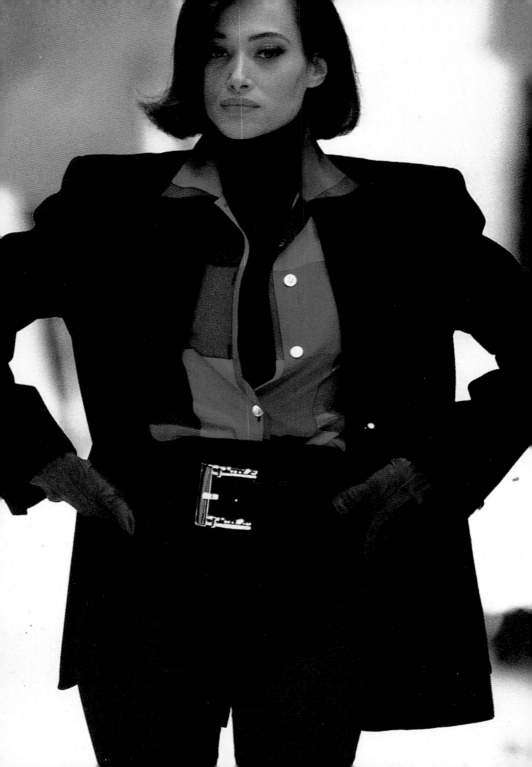

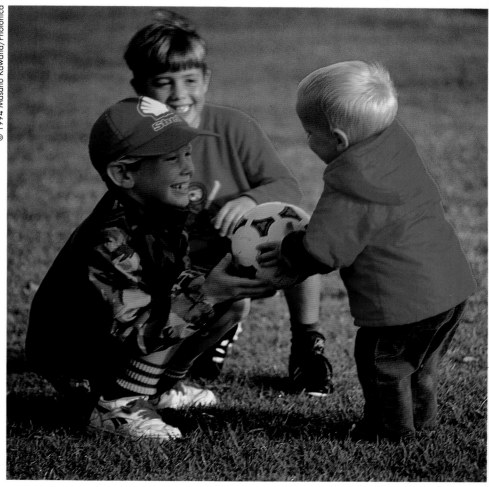

blue-green, and yellow-orange will emerge for the adult woman. Confidence to wear vivid color combinations will increase as women continue to attain more power in the work force. Dark grayish greens and rosy browns are forecast for winter fashion apparel, combined with blue-green, glossy black, and warm metallic for accent.

Children's clothing, always a major player in the fashion industry, has rid itself of pastels and soft colors and contin-

ues the predicted color trend. Vivid, primary hues—blue, red, and yellow—are the favorite colors of children. Bright accents of orange and purple will be added to the uniform of traditional denim blue in the young junior and teenage market, creating a recognizable complement.

The sports fashion industry will continue to use vivid colors, but the neon look of the past is giving way to a more standard brilliant palette. Vying for domi-

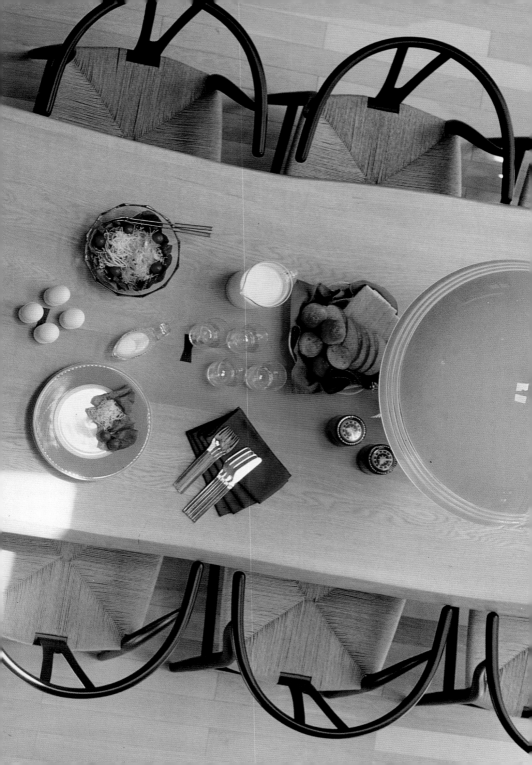

nance in this field, blue-green, violet, and red-orange in full saturation compete with the current reds and blues.

INTERIORS

A major trend in interior color is yellow-orange or saffron, in full saturation as well as in warm, full-bodied tints. This hue will be seen on walls and wall-coverings, ceilings, and window treatments. Yellow-orange creates a warm and welcoming environment and conveys elegance when combined with rich blue-violets, deep blues, and off-white creamy accents. It replaces the flat light yellows and pale tints of the past. Home interiors, eating areas, and restaurant interiors will use variations of this energizing warm yellow hue.

Blues in regal and rich jewel tones, which include blue-greens and blue-violets, will be seen in interiors as well as in fall fashions and automobiles. Pale blues and greens will not be viewed as restful, but icy and unfriendly. Pastels with warm undertones and medium values are replacing the dull gray-greens and grayish blues of the eighties.

Neutrals will be warm to soft red-browns. Deeper tones and values of terra-cotta—a result of the influence of the ongoing Southwest, "natural" trend—are out in front. The boring, sandy neutrals of the past will be replaced with reddish desert tans, highlighted by shades of earthy reds, blues, and greens.

Pine, beech, and natural cherry dominate the interior wood color palette. These off-white and pale yellow woods work well in combination with brightly colored, multipatterned carpets and upholstery. This light flooring and furniture gives a spaciousness to small and large rooms.

Textiles, related fabrics, and floor coverings will center on analogous combinations from the vivid hues of red, green, blue, and yellow-orange. A coordination of these interior elements enables the designer to create an interesting and unifying assortment of textures and schemes. Rather than one color throughout the design of a living area or other interior space, more options are now available.

THE IMPORTANCE OF COLOR FORECASTS AND COLOR TRENDS

Color change affects thousands of industries and also affects artists, craftspeople, manufacturers, suppliers, vendors, and support services from the drawing boards and computers to the home or place of business. A new color or color scheme gives new life to an old product. It also gives life to a number of collateral industries responsible for introducing and maintaining the latest "in" look.

The world economy depends on product viability as well as product "buyability." If the product sells, it is certain that the color forecasting and therefore color trends played a large part in that sale and perhaps may have defined the color trends for the decade.

Process Color Conversion Chart

Color No.	Cyan C	Magenta M	Yellow Y	Black K
1	0	100	100	45
2	0	100	100	25
3	0	100	100	15
4	0	100	100	0
5	0	85	70	0
6	0	65	50	0
7	0	45	30	0
8	0	20	10	0
9	0	90	80	45
10	0	90	80	25
11	0	90	80	15
12	0	90	80	0
13	0	70	65	0
14	0	55	50	0
15	0	40	35	0
16	0	20	20	0
17	0	60	100	45
18	0	60	100	25
19	0	60	100	15
20	0	60	100	0
21	0	50	80	0
22	0	40	60	0
23	0	25	40	0
24	0	15	20	0
25	0	40	100	45
26	0	40	100	25
27	0	40	100	15
28	0	40	100	0
29	0	30	80	0
30	0	25	60	0
31	0	15	40	0
32	0	10	20	0
33	0	0	100	45
34	0	0	100	25
35	0	0	100	15
36	0	0	100	0
37	0	0	80	0
38	0	0	60	0
39	0	0	40	0
40	0	0	25	0
41	60	0	100	45
42	60	0	100	25
43	60	0	100	15
44	60	0	100	0
45	50	0	80	0
46	35	0	60	0
47	25	0	40	0
48	12	0	20	0
49	100	0	90	45
50	100	0	90	25
51	100	0	90	15
52	100	0	90	0
53	80	0	75	0
54	60	0	55	0
55	45	0	35	0
56	25	0	20	0
57	100	0	40	45
58	100	0	40	25
59	100	0	40	15
60	100	0	40	0
61	80	0	30	0
62	60	0	25	0
63	45	0	20	0
64	25	0	10	0
65	100	60	0	45
66	100	60	0	25
67	100	60	0	15
68	100	60	0	0
69	85	50	0	0
70	65	40	0	0
71	50	25	0	0
72	30	15	0	0
73	100	90	0	45
74	100	90	0	25
75	100	90	0	15
76	100	90	0	0
77	85	80	0	0
78	75	65	0	0
79	60	55	0	0
80	45	40	0	0
81	80	100	0	45
82	80	100	0	25
83	80	100	0	15
84	80	100	0	0
85	65	85	0	0
86	55	65	0	0
87	40	50	0	0
88	25	30	0	0
89	40	100	0	45
90	40	100	0	25
91	40	100	0	15
92	40	100	0	0
93	35	80	0	0
94	25	60	0	0
95	20	40	0	0
96	10	20	0	0
97	0	0	0	10
98	0	0	0	20
99	0	0	0	30
100	0	0	0	35
101	0	0	0	45
102	0	0	0	55
103	0	0	0	65
104	0	0	0	75
105	0	0	0	85
106	0	0	0	100

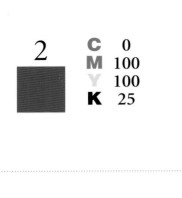

2
C	0
M	100
Y	100
K	25

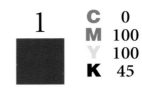

1
C	0
M	100
Y	100
K	45

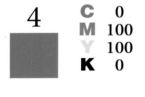

4
C	0
M	100
Y	100
K	0

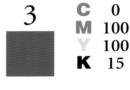

3
C	0
M	100
Y	100
K	15

6
C	0
M	65
Y	50
K	0

5
C	0
M	85
Y	70
K	0

8
C	0
M	20
Y	10
K	0

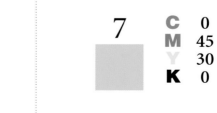

7
C	0
M	45
Y	30
K	0

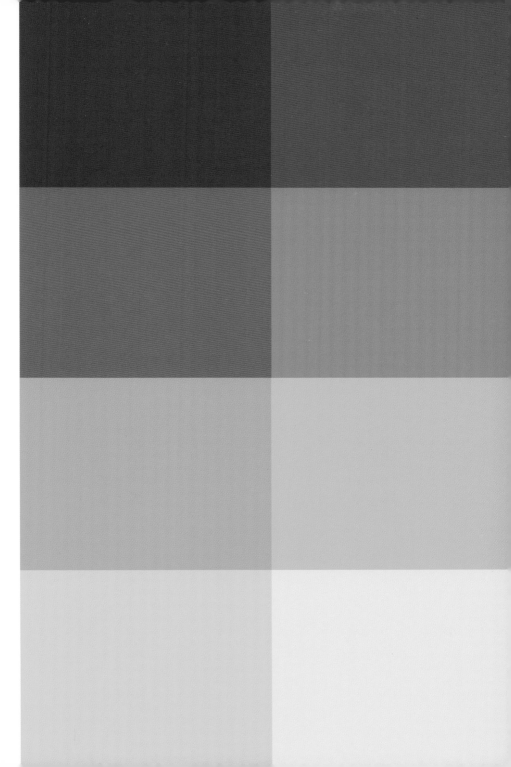

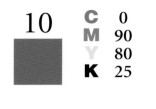

10

C	0
M	90
Y	80
K	25

9

C	0
M	90
Y	80
K	45

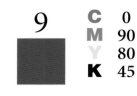

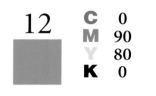

12

C	0
M	90
Y	80
K	0

11

C	0
M	90
Y	80
K	15

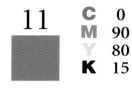

14

C	0
M	55
Y	50
K	0

13

C	0
M	70
Y	65
K	0

16

C	0
M	20
Y	20
K	0

15

C	0
M	40
Y	35
K	0

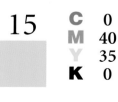

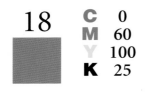

18   C 0
      M 60
      Y 100
      K 25

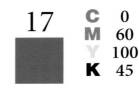

17   C 0
      M 60
      Y 100
      K 45

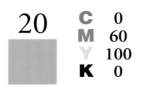

20   C 0
      M 60
      Y 100
      K 0

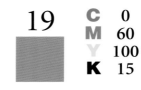

19   C 0
      M 60
      Y 100
      K 15

22   C 0
      M 40
      Y 60
      K 0

21   C 0
      M 50
      Y 80
      K 0

24   C 0
      M 15
      Y 20
      K 0

23   C 0
      M 25
      Y 40
      K 0

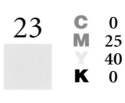

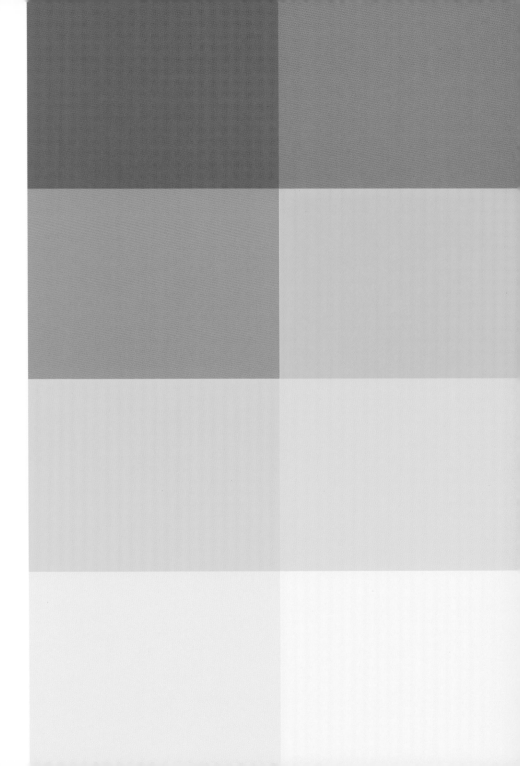

26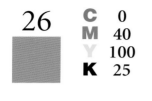
C 0
M 40
Y 100
K 25

25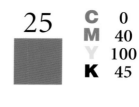
C 0
M 40
Y 100
K 45

28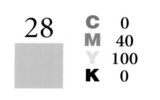
C 0
M 40
Y 100
K 0

27
C 0
M 40
Y 100
K 15

30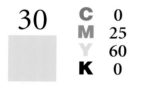
C 0
M 25
Y 60
K 0

29
C 0
M 30
Y 80
K 0

32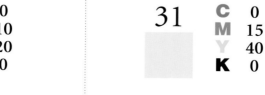
C 0
M 10
Y 20
K 0

31
C 0
M 15
Y 40
K 0

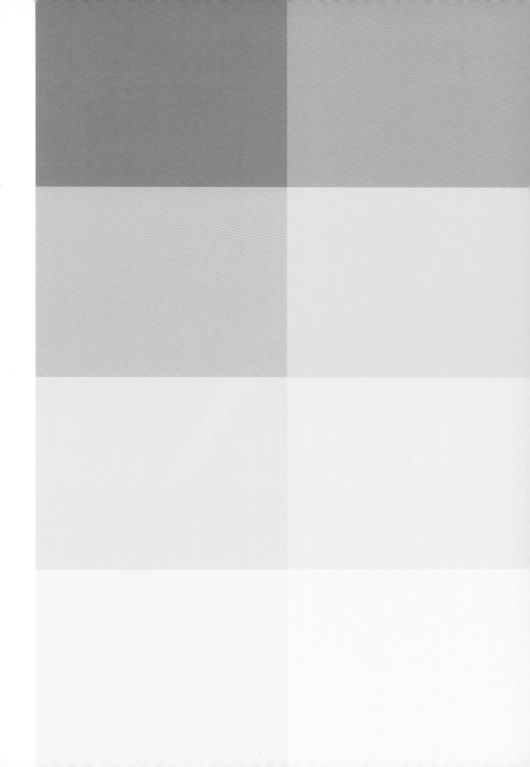

34	C	0
	M	0
	Y	100
	K	25

33	C	0
	M	0
	Y	100
	K	45

36	C	0
	M	0
	Y	100
	K	0

35	C	0
	M	0
	Y	100
	K	15

38	C	0
	M	0
	Y	60
	K	0

37	C	0
	M	0
	Y	80
	K	0

40	C	0
	M	0
	Y	25
	K	0

39	C	0
	M	0
	Y	40
	K	0

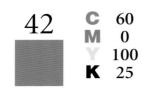

42

C	60
M	0
Y	100
K	25

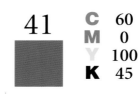

41

C	60
M	0
Y	100
K	45

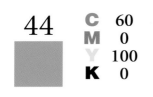

44

C	60
M	0
Y	100
K	0

43

C	60
M	0
Y	100
K	15

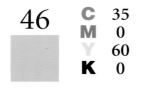

46

C	35
M	0
Y	60
K	0

45

C	50
M	0
Y	80
K	0

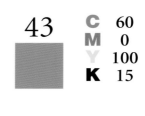

48

C	12
M	0
Y	20
K	0

47

C	25
M	0
Y	40
K	0

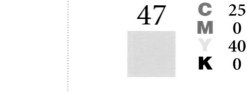

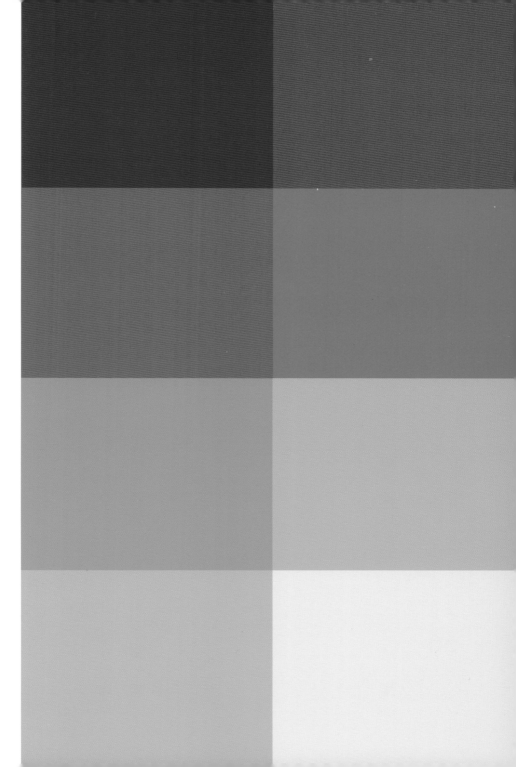

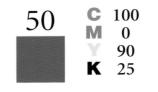

50

C 100
M 0
Y 90
K 25

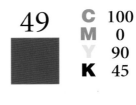

49

C 100
M 0
Y 90
K 45

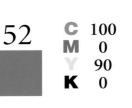

52

C 100
M 0
Y 90
K 0

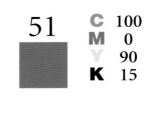

51

C 100
M 0
Y 90
K 15

54

C 60
M 0
Y 55
K 0

53

C 80
M 0
Y 75
K 0

56

C 25
M 0
Y 20
K 0

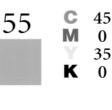

55

C 45
M 0
Y 35
K 0

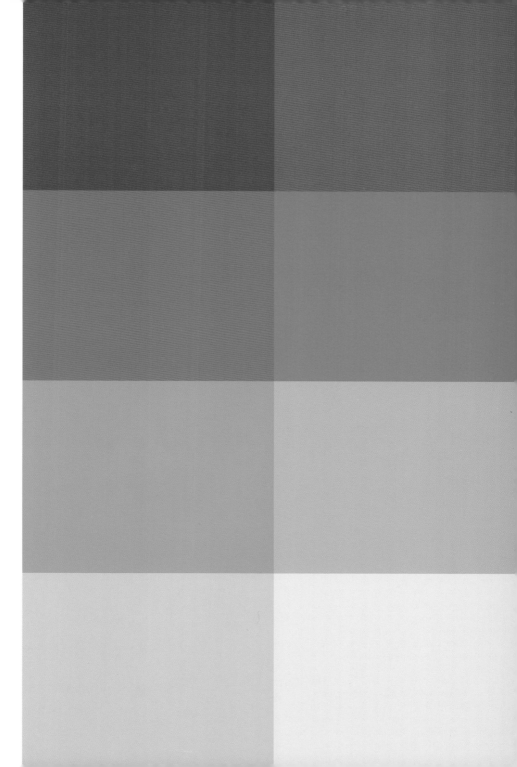

58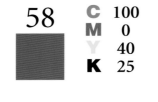

C 100
M 0
Y 40
K 25

57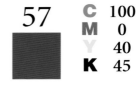

C 100
M 0
Y 40
K 45

60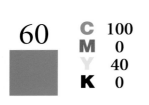

C 100
M 0
Y 40
K 0

59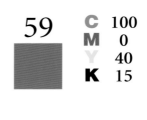

C 100
M 0
Y 40
K 15

62

C 60
M 0
Y 25
K 0

61

C 80
M 0
Y 30
K 0

64

C 25
M 0
Y 10
K 0

63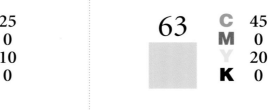

C 45
M 0
Y 20
K 0

66   **C** 100   **M** 60   **Y** 0   **K** 25

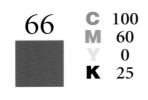

65   **C** 100   **M** 60   **Y** 0   **K** 45

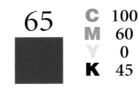

68   **C** 100   **M** 60   **Y** 0   **K** 0

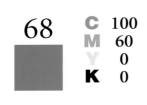

67   **C** 100   **M** 60   **Y** 0   **K** 15

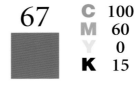

70   **C** 65   **M** 40   **Y** 0   **K** 0

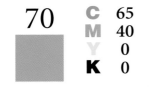

69   **C** 85   **M** 50   **Y** 0   **K** 0

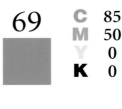

72   **C** 30   **M** 15   **Y** 0   **K** 0

71   **C** 50   **M** 25   **Y** 0   **K** 0

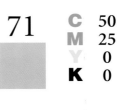

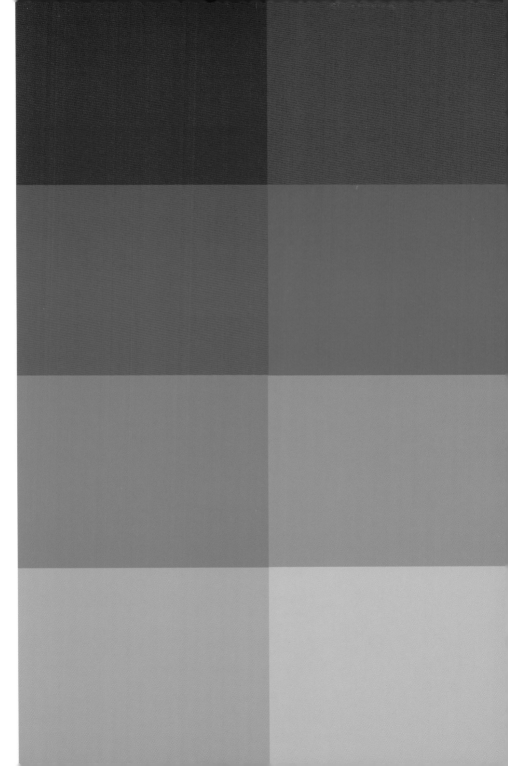

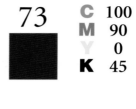

74

C 100
M 90
Y 0
K 25

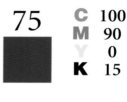

73

C 100
M 90
Y 0
K 45

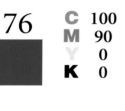

76

C 100
M 90
Y 0
K 0

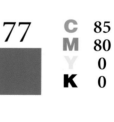

75

C 100
M 90
Y 0
K 15

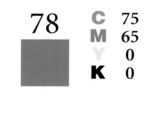

78

C 75
M 65
Y 0
K 0

77

C 85
M 80
Y 0
K 0

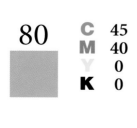

80

C 45
M 40
Y 0
K 0

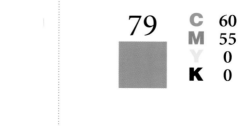

79

C 60
M 55
Y 0
K 0

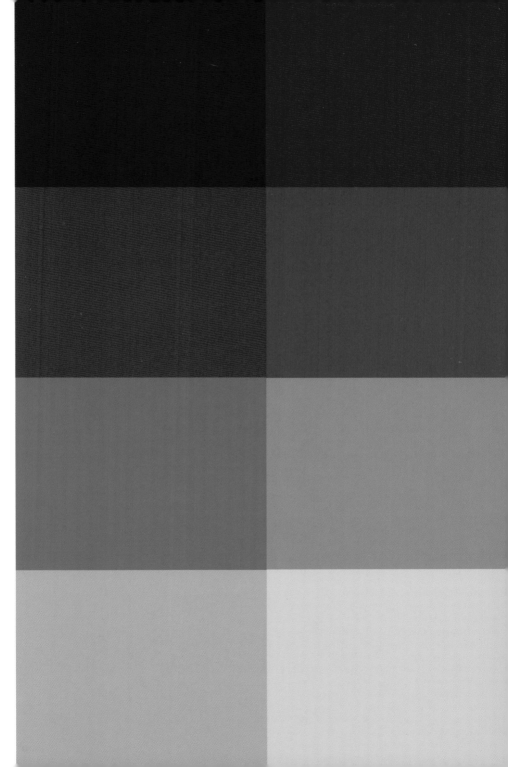

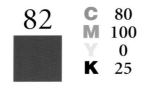

82   C   80
       M   100
       Y   0
       K   25

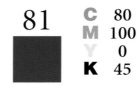

81   C   80
       M   100
       Y   0
       K   45

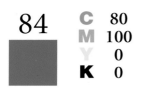

84   C   80
       M   100
       Y   0
       K   0

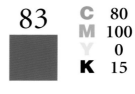

83   C   80
       M   100
       Y   0
       K   15

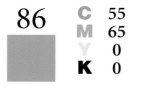

86   C   55
       M   65
       Y   0
       K   0

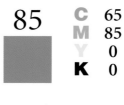

85   C   65
       M   85
       Y   0
       K   0

88   C   25
       M   30
       Y   0
       K   0

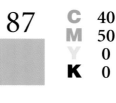

87   C   40
       M   50
       Y   0
       K   0

90

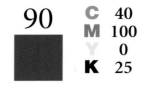

C	40
M	100
Y	0
K	25

89

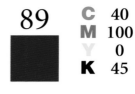

C	40
M	100
Y	0
K	45

92

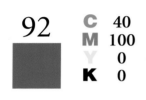

C	40
M	100
Y	0
K	0

91

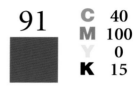

C	40
M	100
Y	0
K	15

94

C	25
M	60
Y	0
K	0

93

C	35
M	80
Y	0
K	0

96

C	10
M	20
Y	0
K	0

95

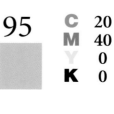

C	20
M	40
Y	0
K	0

98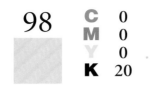

C 0
M 0
Y 0
K 20

97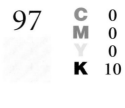

C 0
M 0
Y 0
K 10

100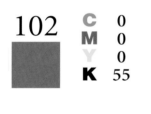

C 0
M 0
Y 0
K 35

99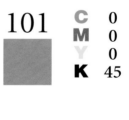

C 0
M 0
Y 0
K 30

102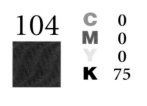

C 0
M 0
Y 0
K 55

101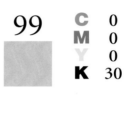

C 0
M 0
Y 0
K 45

104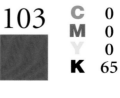

C 0
M 0
Y 0
K 75

103

C 0
M 0
Y 0
K 65

Photography Credits

Photography courtesy of :

Ford Motor Company
Research and Engineering Center
P.O. Box 2053
Dearborn, MI 48121-2053

FPG International
32 Union Square East
New York, NY 10003-3295
212-777-4210

Sam Gray Photography
23 Westwood Road
Wellesley, MA 02181
617-237-2711

Geoffrey Gross
40 West 27th Street
12th Floor
New York, NY 10001
212-685-8850

Hing and Norton
24 West 30th Street, 8th Floor
New York, NY 10001
212-679-5933

Hornick/Rivlin Studio
25 Drydock Avenue
Boston, MA 02210
617-482-8614

The Image Bank
111 Fifth Avenue
New York, NY 10003
212-529-6700

Index Stock Photography, Inc.
126 Fifth Avenue
New York, NY 10011
212-929-4644

Kravet Fabrics — Fabrics, Wallcoverings,
Trimmings, Furniture
225 Central Avenue South
Bethpage, NY 11714
516-293-2000

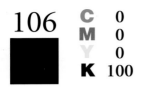

106   C 0
  M 0
  Y 0
  K 100

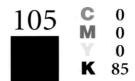

105   C 0
  M 0
  Y 0
  K 85

Mercedes-Benz of North America, Inc.
One Mercedes Drive
P.O. Box 350
Montvale, NJ 07645-0350

Metropolitan Home
1633 Broadway
New York, NY 10019

Photonica New York
141 Fifth Avenue
Suite 8 South
New York, NY 10010
212-505-9000

Pottery Barn
Williams-Sonoma, Inc.
100 North Point Street
San Francisco, CA 94133
415-421-7900

Schumacher
79 Madison Avenue
New York, NY 10016
212-213-7908

Stock Imagery
711 Kalamath Street
Denver, CO 80204
1-800-288-3686

The Stock Market
360 Park Avenue, South
New York, NY 10010
212-684-7878

Tony Stone Worldwide
233 East Ontario Street
Suite 1200
Chicago, IL 60611
1-800-234-7800

Superstock
Deerwood Park
Jacksonville, FL 32256
904-565-0066

Dan Wagner Photography
231 29th Street
Suite #307
New York, NY 10001
212-279-4042